home sewn
nursery

home sewn nursery

TOYS, CLOTHES AND FURNISHINGS
FOR A BEAUTIFUL BABY'S ROOM

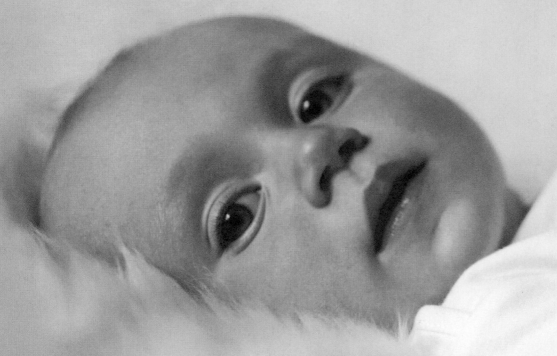

Tina Barrett

First published 2012 by
Guild of Master Craftsman Publications Ltd
Castle Place, 166 High Street, Lewes,
East Sussex BN7 1XU

ISBN 978-1-86108-835-2

Publisher: Jonathan Bailey

Production Manager: Jim Bulley

Managing Editor: Gerrie Purcell

Senior Project Editor: Virginia Brehaut

Copy Editor: Rachel Parkinson

Managing Art Editor: Gilda Pacitti

Photographer: Chris Gloag

Colour origination by GMC Reprographics

Printed and bound in China by 1010 Printing
International Ltd

Contents

Introduction

To stitchers old and new, I hope you will find a host of projects to inspire you within these pages to make for your little loved ones. There is something very special about making clothes and toys for your own precious babies and I would urge anyone to give it a go, even if you don't need to save the pennies.

As a young child, I was extremely fortunate to have two sets of grandmothers who were skilled with needles. My great grandmother, Emily, taught me to knit and embroider whilst my Nan, Irene, who made all our clothes and school dresses, showed me how to cut out fabric, hand sew hems and use a sewing machine. Back in those days I used my very basic skills to cut out dolls' clothes from old pillowcases. I cobbled them together with rudimentary stitches and, more often than not, forgot to finish them.

When I became a teenager and pocket money was tight, I tie-dyed old sheets and made my own clothes and patterns so I could look like the girls in all the teen magazines. Time passed, and it was not until I had my own children that I even thought about dusting off my old sewing machine again.

If you think you can't sew, then this is the book for you. I have tried to keep things simple and the step-by-step photos will guide you through each project so you are never alone.

Lots of the toys and accessories can be made from small amounts of material, so they are ideal for using up scraps of leftover fabric. You could even try recycling old dresses, shirts or pillowcases.

So, whichever project you choose to sew, remember that all the money in the world cannot buy the love you have put into each stitch. And if you have older children, why not share your own skills so that in time, they can pass the love on to their own children?

Happy sewing!

Tina

Out and about

Reversible buggy liner

Keep your buggy clean and mess free with this useful, reversible liner.
Use cotton, polar fleece or oilcloth in bright colours, then simply remove
and pop in the washing machine when it gets a bit grubby.

You will need
- 2 x 40in (1m) contrast fabric in cotton, polar fleece or oilcloth
- 1 pack of contrast bias binding
- 40in (1m) of 2oz (70g) wadding
- Contrast sewing thread
- Sewing machine
- Hand-sewing needle
- Dressmaking shears
- Pins and pincushion
- Tape measure
- Fabric marker or tailor's chalk

Pattern pieces
My liner was made to fit a standard buggy but yours may vary in size so follow the instructions to tailor-fit your own. Measure the height and depth of the buggy's seat. Add these measurements together to calculate the length of the liner. Now measure the width of the seat, which will be the width of the liner. My measurements were 29½ x 16½in (75 x 42cm). No seam allowance is needed because you will be binding the edges. Using these measurements and keeping everything square, cut one out in each contrast fabric and one in wadding. You will have three pieces in total.

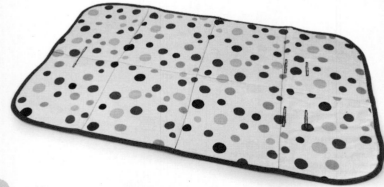

Reversible buggy liner

Step 1
Using the fabric marker or tailor's chalk, draw round the edges of each corner **A** and trim. Now place all layers together in a sandwich with the wadding in the middle. The wrong side of the fabric should face the wadding so the right sides are uppermost. Pin around all the edges.

Step 2
To mark out the quilt lines, measure along the short edge and find the centre point. Use the tailor's chalk or fabric marker to mark this line right down the centre of the liner and pin. Now measure down the long edge and again, find the centre point. Mark across the width as before. Measure down from this line to the bottom and mark the halfway point as before. Repeat above the centre line. You will have marked out eight quilted squares **B**.

Step 3
Using contrast thread, machine-stitch along all the lines **C**.

Step 4
Beginning at the centre of the short edge, fold the bias binding in half and pin it around all the raw edges, sandwiching all the layers between it, then tack **D**. Using contrast thread, topstitch the edging.

Step 5
Measure the position of the harness straps and seat belt buckle and mark onto the liner using the tailor's chalk or fabric marker **E**.

Step 6
Using contrast thread and the buttonhole foot, stitch a long buttonhole along these marks (see page 133). Snip the centres to open **F**.

TOP TIP
Make one side of the liner in oilcloth so you can flip it over at baby's snack times, then wipe clean afterwards for mess-free meals on the go.

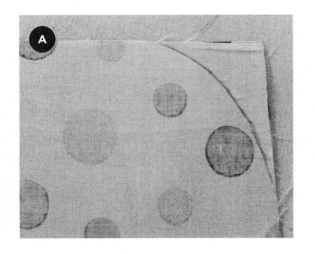

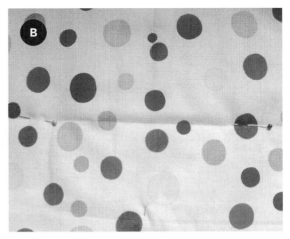

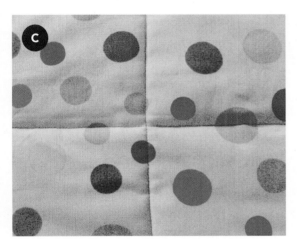

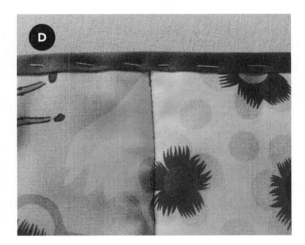

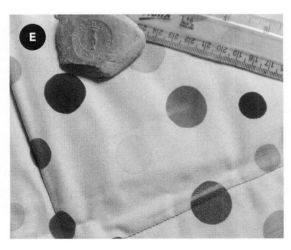

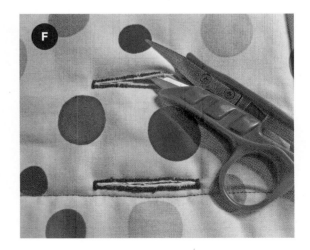

Easy-peasy sunhat

This cute sunhat is so quick and easy to make, I guarantee you could make it in an afternoon. It has a wide brim to protect baby from the strongest of rays and folds down to almost nothing, ensuring you are always prepared for the sun.

You will need
- 20in (50cm) main fabric
- 1 fat quarter of contrast fabric
- Contrast thread for hand-sewing and machine-sewing
- Sewing machine
- Hand-sewing needle
- Dressmaking shears
- Pins and pincushion
- Iron and ironing board

Sizes
To fit 0–6 months [6–12 months: 1–2 years]
Size shown on model: 6–12 months

Pattern pieces
You will need the following pattern pieces from pattern sheet **E**. Trace the pieces onto tracing paper and cut them out. A ½in (1cm) seam allowance is included in all pattern pieces. Use a ½in (1cm) seam allowance throughout the pattern, unless otherwise stated.

1 **CROWN** cut 3 in main fabric. Cut 3 in contrast fabric
2 **BRIM** cut 2 in main fabric

Easy-peasy sunhat

Step 1

Arrange the crown sections into sets of three. With right sides facing, pin and stitch the seams. Press the seams to one side. You will have two half spheres **A**.

Step 2

Join the brim ends to form a circle. With right sides together, pin and stitch **B**. Repeat for second brim piece.

Step 3

With right sides facing, place the two pieces of brim together and stitch around the outer edge. Turn right side out and topstitch around the outer edge **C**.

Step 4

With right sides facing, line up the inner edges of the brim with the hat crown. Pin and stitch. Press the seam towards the crown of the hat **D**.

TOP TIP

If your baby is prone to losing hats, you could add a length of elastic to hook under the chin. Simply cut to length, ensuring it is not too tight and stitch the ends to the inside edge where the brim meets the crown.

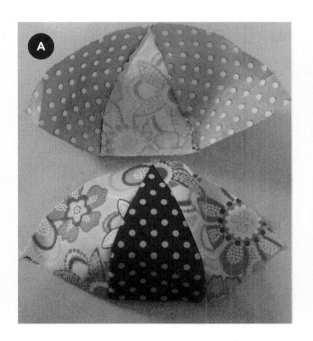

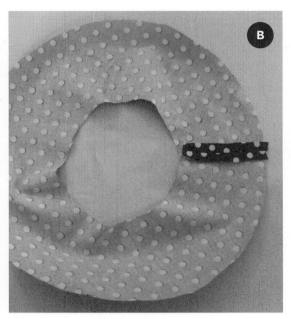

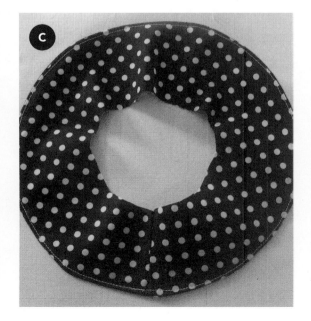

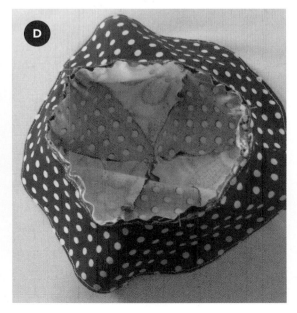

Changing bag

This ingenuous nappy bag is lined with oilcloth so the inside is totally waterproof, which makes it perfect for storing wet wipes and cream. Simply unfasten the sides and open it out for a ready-made changing mat.

You will need
- 40in (1m) main fabric
- 20in (50cm) contrast oilcloth
- 2 large decorative buttons
- 40in (1m) white hook-and-loop tape
- Tube of strong textile glue (I use Gutermann textile glue HT2)
- Contrast sewing thread
- Sewing machine
- Hand-sewing needle
- Dressmaking shears
- Pins and pincushion
- Tape measure
- Fabric marker or tailor's chalk

Pattern pieces
You will need to cut pieces of fabric in the sizes below. A ½in (1cm) seam allowance is included in the measurements. Use a ½in (1cm) seam allowance throughout the pattern, unless otherwise stated. The finished bag measures 16 x 28in (41 x 71cm).

BAG 17 x 29in (43 x 74cm).
Cut 1 in main fabric. Cut 1 in oilcloth
POCKETS 17 x 9½in (43 x 24cm).
Cut 2 in main fabric
HANDLES 8 x 30in (20 x 76cm).
Cut 2 in main fabric

Changing bag

Step 1

Fold the outer edges of each strap towards the centre by ½in (1cm) and press **A**. Fold in half lengthwise and press again. Machine-stitch the seam and then topstitch the opposite edge **B**.

Step 2

Place the two pocket pieces together with right sides facing. Machine-stitch both long edges, keeping the side edges open. Turn right side out and press. Then topstitch the top edge **C**.

Step 3

Fold the main body of the bag in half. Pin and tack the pocket onto the front. Open the bag out and machine-stitch the pocket in place along the bottom long edge. Find the centre of the pocket and mark a line from top to bottom. Machine-stitch along it to make two pockets. Sew a button to each pocket top **D**.

Step 4

To assemble the bag, make a big sandwich as follows: place the bag body and oilcloth lining together with right sides facing. Now fold the handles in half and position at opposite ends of the bag along the short edge. Make sure they are facing downwards so the loops face towards each other. Slide them into the middle part of the sandwich and pin the ends in place **E**.

Step 5

Pin and machine-stitch around all edges, beginning halfway down the long edge on the back of the bag (the part without the pocket). Leave a 4in (10cm) opening for turning. It is a good idea to double-stitch the handles for strength. Turn the bag right side out through the opening. Press, on the fabric side, and then close the opening with slipstitch **F** (see page 136).

Step 6

Fold the bag in half with handles matching. Measure and cut two pieces of hook-and-loop tape, approximately 15in (38cm) in length. Open the bag out. Apply the textile glue to the back of each strip and then position along the outside edges of the oilcloth lining and stick firmly in place.

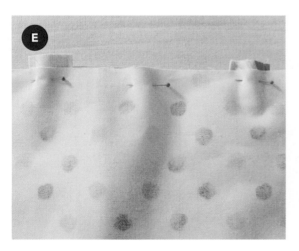

Earflap hat

This earflap jester hat can easily be made in a single afternoon and is an ideal starter project for those new to dressmaking. I have used polar fleece, which is warm to wear and doesn't fray so you don't even need to neaten the seams.

You will need
- 20in (50cm) main polar fleece
- 20in (50cm) contrast polar fleece
- Contrast sewing thread
- Sewing machine
- Hand-sewing needle
- Dressmaking shears
- Pins and pincushion

Size
To fit 2–3 years

Pattern pieces
You will need the following pattern piece from pattern sheet **C**. Trace the piece onto tracing paper and cut it out. A ½in (1cm) seam allowance is included. Use a ½in (1cm) seam allowance throughout the pattern, unless otherwise stated.

3 **HAT** cut 1 in main fleece.
   Cut 1 in contrast fleece
TASSELS 2½ x 5in (6 x 13cm) pieces.
Cut 4 in main fleece. Cut 2 in contrast fleece

Earflap hat

Step 1

With right sides facing, pin the main and contrast fleece together. Using a ¼in (6mm) seam allowance, machine-stitch along lower earflap edge **A**. Turn right side out and topstitch along the lower edge.

Step 2

Fold the hat in half, pin and machine-stitch the rear seam **B**. Using the template as a guide, open out the hat with wrong sides facing and mark the jester points with pins. Stitch along the line **C**. Trim the excess fabric and turn right side out.

Step 3

Take two main pieces and one contrast piece for each tassel. Snip along both sides of each piece so the cuts almost meet in the middle **D**.

Step 4

Place the pieces on top of each other in a sandwich, alternating the colours. Roll up and tie with a small strip of main fabric. Using a hand-sewing needle and contrast thread, secure the bundle through the middle with a few stitches **E**. Then attach a tassel to each point with small, firm stitches **F**.

TOP TIP
When tackling layers of fleece, adjust your presser foot tension so it is at its loosest. This ensures smooth stitching and makes it easier to feed the fabric through.

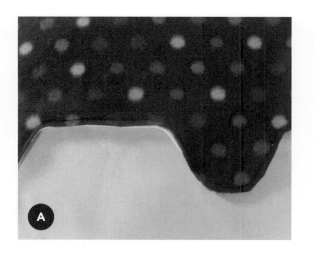

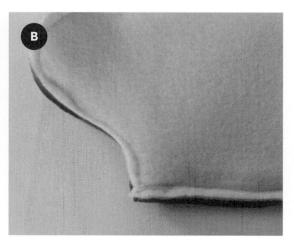

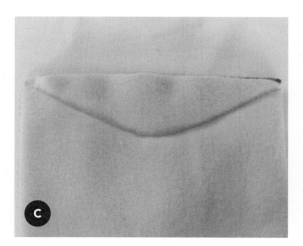

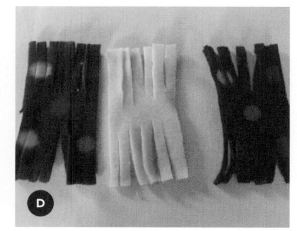

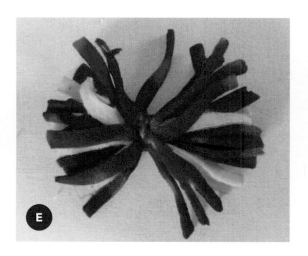

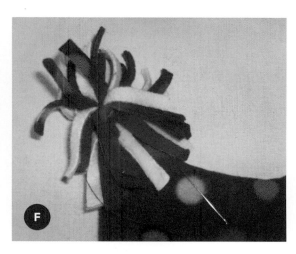

Nursery accessories

Baby's cot quilt

Simple patchwork makes this bright quilt so easy to make. Mix up all your
leftover fabrics to make a unique cover just for your baby. The easy square
patchwork pieces make great practice for those new to quilting.

You will need
- 5 x 20in (50cm) pieces of bright fabric
- 40in (1m) fabric for the edging
- 40in (1m) of 2oz (70g) wadding
- 40in (1m) backing material
- Contrast sewing thread
- Sewing machine
- Hand-sewing needle
- Dressmaking shears
- Pins and pincushion
- Iron and ironing board
- Rotary cutter and board or
  flat ruler and sharp scissors

Pattern pieces
PATCHES Cut 30 squares 6½ x 6½in
(17 x 17cm). Cut 6 in each colourway.

Baby's cot quilt

Step 1
Assemble all the squares together in rows of five, mixing up the colours. Pin and machine-stitch the first row. Press the seams open. When you have assembled two rows, machine-stitch both rows together. Press the seams open as you go **A**.

Step 2
Continue to assemble the patches in rows and carefully stitch each row to the main body of the fabric until you have used all the squares. The quilt will be five squares wide and six squares long.

Step 3
Next, sandwich the piece of wadding between the patchwork upper and the backing fabric. Hand-tack around all edges (see page 133) and trim the bottom two layers to the size of the upper piece **B**.

Step 4
Cut lengths of 4in (10cm) bias strips from your edging fabric as follows. Locate the bias of your fabric by folding diagonally so that the straight edge on the crosswise grain is parallel to the selvedge. Press the fabric along the fold, open it out and, using the crease as a guide, mark parallel lines 4in (10cm) apart. Cut along the marked lines to create your bias strips. Cut enough strips to reach around all four edges of the quilt.

Step 5
Join the bias strips together as follows: Place one strip right side up and vertical. Lay the second strip horizontally across the top edge of the first with wrong side upwards. Pin diagonally across the corner edge **C**. Stitch across the pin line, trim the excess seam allowance, open out the strip and press **D**. Continue in this way until all the strips are joined.

TOP TIP
Don't miss out the tacking stage when making your quilt. It will make the edging process much easier.

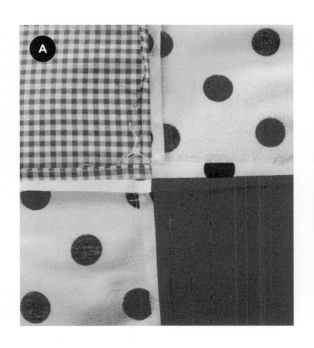

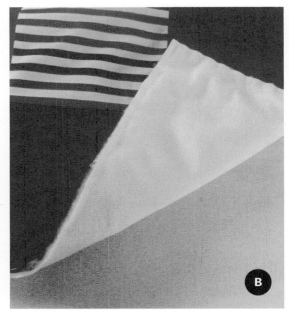

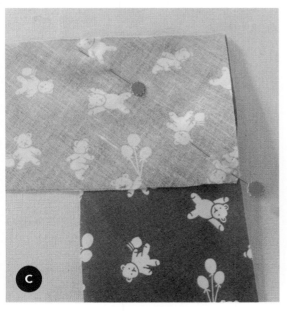

Step 6

Beginning in the centre of one short edge of the quilt, pin the edging strip, right sides together, around the edges. Mitre the corners and pin the mitre **E**. You will have a triangle of excess fabric at each corner but do not worry about it at this stage. Ensure you have a 2in (5cm) excess at the beginning and end of the edging strip.

Step 7

To join the ends of the strips, butt the edges together, folding back the excess **F**. Pin and machine-stitch the seam. Trim the excess allowance, open seam and press. Use a ⅝in (1.5cm) seam allowance and machine-stitch around all edges **G**. Stop short of each corner by 1in (2.5cm).

Step 8

Fold the edging over to the wrong side of the quilt, fold up the seam allowance and pin and press the edges **H**. Tuck the mitred corners in at front and back as shown. Slipstitch around the edging on the wrong side of the quilt. Slipstitch the mitred corners on the front and back (see page 136 for slipstitch).

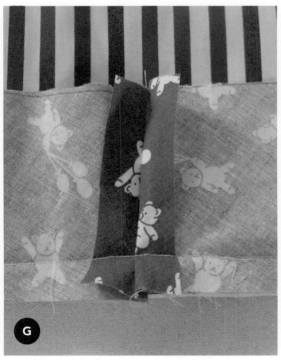

Jungle wall art

Practise your appliqué with these fun jungle animal wall hangings. These are very simple shapes so it's an ideal project for beginners. The appliquéd square is attached to an art canvas for an instant, ready-to-hang work of art.

You will need

- 3 x squares of calico 10 x 10in (25 x 25cm)
- 3 x stretched art canvases 8 x 8in (20 x 20cm)
- Small pieces contrast fabric for each animal
- Small pieces contrast fabric for the appliqué
- 5 small buttons for eyes
- Double-sided fusible interfacing
- Contrast embroidery and sewing thread
- Staple gun or glue gun and glue sticks
- Sewing machine
- Hand-sewing needle
- Dressmaking shears
- Pins and pincushion
- Iron and ironing board

Pattern pieces

You will need the following pattern pieces from pattern sheet Ⓐ. Trace the pieces onto tracing paper and cut them out. There is no seam allowance included in these pieces.

4 CROCODILE BODY cut 1 in main fabric. Cut 1 in interfacing

5 CROCODILE EYE cut 1 in contrast fabric. Cut 1 in interfacing

6 CROCODILE EYELID cut 1 in contrast fabric. Cut 1 in interfacing

7 GIRAFFE BODY cut 1 in main fabric. Cut 1 in interfacing

8 GIRAFFE MUZZLE cut 1 in contrast fabric. Cut 1 in interfacing

9 GIRAFFE EARS cut 2 in contrast fabric. Cut 2 in interfacing

10 LION BODY cut 1 in main fabric. Cut 1 in interfacing

11 LION MANE cut 1 in contrast fabric. Cut 1 in interfacing

12 LION TAIL cut 1 in main fabric. Cut 1 in interfacing

13 TAIL TIP cut 1 in contrast fabric. Cut 1 in interfacing

14 LION PAWS cut 2 in contrast fabric. Cut 2 in interfacing

Jungle wall art

Step 1
Assemble the template pieces for each animal and position them in the centre of the calico square. Follow the numerical order of the template labels for each animal when positioning them: 4–6 for the crocodile, 7–9 for the giraffe and 10–14 for the lion. When all the pieces are assembled, iron on the interfacing to fix in place (see page 134 for more on appliqué).

Step 2
Appliqué the crocodile by working a zigzag stitch around the outer edge of the silhouette. Refer to the template to pick out detail lines. Sew on a button for the eye. Embroider the nose and mouth in backstitch, using contrast embroidery thread **A**.

Step 3
Appliqué the giraffe in the same way as the crocodile. Use a sewing needle and embroidery thread to work running stitch around the muzzle and ears. Work the two horns in backstitch. Sew on two buttons for the eyes **B**.

Step 4
Work a zigzag stitch around the outer edge of the lion, as before. I used brown felt for the lion's mane, tail and feet. Use a sewing needle and embroidery thread to work curved rows of running stitch around the mane, tail and feet. Work the mouth in backstitch. Sew on two buttons for eyes **C**.

Step 5
Neaten all four sides of each calico square and press. Stretch the calico square over the canvas base, mitring each corner. Attach to the back of the frame using a staple gun or a glue gun **D**.

TOP TIP
When working around the edges don't worry too much about the neatness of your zigzag stitch. Just concentrate on obtaining a result you are happy with.

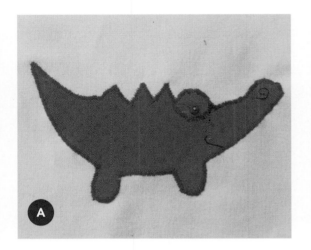

Caterpillar toy

This cuddly caterpillar is made from seven stuffed discs in a combination of fleece, cotton and satin ribbon for a tactile toy. Hook the handy ribbon loop on to your buggy or carry-chair so he can travel everywhere with you and baby.

You will need
- 6 fat quarters of brightly coloured cotton fabric
- 1 square of 9 x 9in (23 x 23cm) felt or polar fleece
- Small piece of red felt for cheeks
- Small amount of blue wool for antennae
- 40in (1m) length of 1in (2.5cm) red satin ribbon
- 2 small bells (optional)
- 10in (25cm) thin elastic (slightly thicker than shirring elastic)
- Polyester toy filling
- Black thread for hand-sewing
- Contrast thread for machine sewing
- Sewing machine
- Tapestry needle
- Hand-sewing needle
- Dressmaking shears
- Pins and pincushion
- Iron and ironing board

Pattern pieces
You will need the following pattern pieces from pattern sheet ❀. Trace the pieces onto tracing paper and cut them out. A ½in (1cm) seam allowance is included in all pattern pieces. Use a ½in (1cm) seam allowance throughout the pattern, unless otherwise stated.

15 **BODY** cut 12 in 6 contrast fabrics. Cut 2 in pink felt or fleece
16 **CHEEKS** cut 2 in red felt

Caterpillar toy

Step 1
Cut and arrange the discs in pairs **A**.
Cut 12 pieces of satin ribbon approximately
2in (5cm) in length. Take the first two pieces,
fold in half and pin to the right side of the first
disc with the loops pointing towards the
centre of the disc **B**.

Step 2
Pin the second corresponding disc on top,
right sides facing. Machine-stitch around the
disc, leaving a 1in (2.5cm) opening for turning
and stuffing **C**.

Step 3
Turn the disc right side out and stuff firmly.
Close the opening with firm slipstitching **D**
(see page 136). Repeat for the remaining five
discs that make up the body.

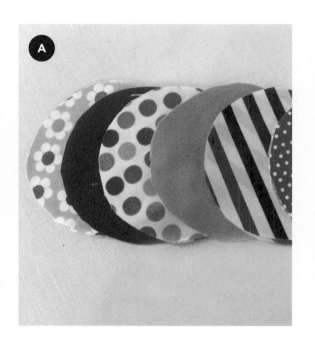

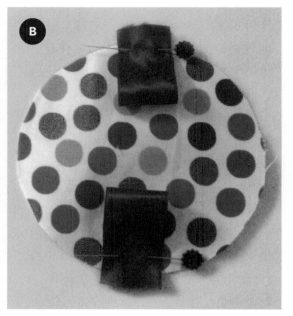

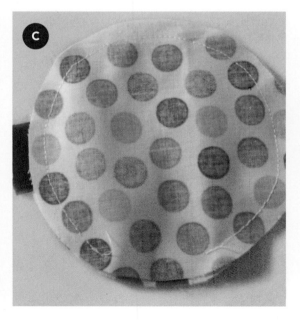

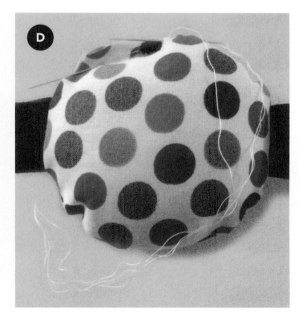

Step 4

Assemble the body pieces into a tower. Thread a tapestry needle with the elastic and push the needle through the centre of all discs. Now thread the bells onto the elastic and push the needle back up through all the discs, to come out where you started **E**. Tie off the elastic tightly. Stitch the elastic into the top disc to secure and snip ends.

Step 5

To make the caterpillar's face, take one of the pink fleece discs and position the red felt circles on to the disc. Use blanket stitch or backstitch to sew the cheeks onto the face with contrast thread. Using black thread, work the mouth in backstitch. Work two French knots for the eyes **F**.

Step 6

Cut an 8in (20cm) length of satin ribbon for the top loop. Fold in half and pin at the top of the face, with the loop pointing downwards **G**. Place the corresponding fleece disc on top and stitch around the sandwich as before, leaving a 1in (2.5cm) opening across the chin. Turn right-side out and stuff. Close the opening with firm slipstitch. Sew the head onto the body using firm stitches **H**. Make two antennae by plaiting or twisting 2in (5cm) strands of blue wool. Tie a knot at the end of each and sew to the top of the caterpillar's head using small firm stitches.

TOP TIP
I have added bells to the end of the caterpillar's tail. These need to be very firmly attached for safety reasons. If you'd prefer, insert the bells inside one of the body discs before closing the opening with firm slipstitch.

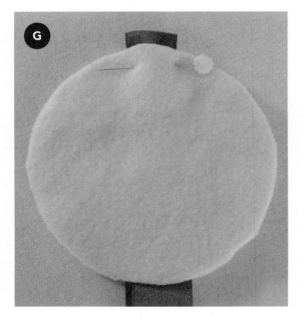

Froggie hooded towel

Bath time is so much fun with Froggie. Just slip his hood over your toddler's head and wrap up in a cute bundle for fast drying without the fuss. Take to the beach or swimming pool too for an instant bath robe to keep the shivers away.

You will need
- 2¼yd (2m) green towelling
- Small pieces of white, black, yellow and red felt
- Small amount of polyester toy filling
- 5yd (4.5m) bias binding
- Contrast sewing thread
- Sewing machine
- Hand-sewing needle
- Iron and ironing board
- Dressmaking shears
- Pins and pincushion

Pattern pieces
You will need the following pattern pieces from pattern sheet **B**. Trace the pieces onto tracing paper and cut them out. A ½in (1cm) seam allowance is included in all pattern pieces. Use a ½in (1cm) seam allowance throughout the pattern, unless otherwise stated.

17 HOOD PIECE cut 3 in towelling
18 EYES cut 2 in white felt
19 PUPILS cut 2 in black felt
20 CHEEKS cut 2 in red felt
21 CROWN cut 2 in yellow felt
MAIN TOWEL 40 x 40in (1 x 1m).
Cut 1 in towelling

Froggie hooded towel

Step 1
Take one of the hood pieces and lay the felt features onto the face **A**. Stitch the eyes and cheeks around the edges (see page 134 for more on appliqué). Work a red line for the smiley mouth in chain stitch **B**.

Step 2
Pin the two pieces of crown together. With a ¼in (6mm) seam allowance, machine-stitch around all edges, leaving the bottom edge open. Stuff firmly with toy stuffing **C**.

Step 3
With right sides facing, pin the frog face to one of the blank face pieces, right sides together. Machine-stitch along the lower straight edge. Turn right side out and topstitch along this edge **D**.

Step 4
With right sides facing, pin the top layers of the hood together with the third blank face piece, sandwiching the crown at the top of the head **E**.

Step 5
Stitch around the top of the face, crown and eyes leaving the lower straight edge open. Turn right-side out. Centre the hood along one edge of the towel body and pin in place. Machine-stitch the seam.

Step 6
Attach the bias binding by folding in half lengthways and pinning around all the square edges of the towel. Begin and end at the centre point of the hood seam. Mitre each corner and tack everything in place **F**. Machine-stitch the binding around all edges.

TOP TIP
I've hand-sewn the eyes and cheeks but you could also use a machine zigzag stitch around the edges of the motifs.

Baby bibs

These cute bibs can be made in an afternoon. There is a super quick plain version with functional oilcloth backing and an appliqué version for those who want to spend a little more time creating a mealtime masterpiece.

You will need

- 20in (50cm) each of fabric and oilcloth for the plain bib
- 20in (50cm) each of main fabric and contrast fabric for the appliqué bib
- Fat quarter of contrast fabric and a small amount of black felt for the appliqué bib
- Double-sided fusible interfacing
- Contrast sewing thread
- Sewing machine
- Hand-sewing needle and black embroidery thread
- Dressmaking shears
- Pins and pincushion
- Iron and ironing board
- Rotary cutter and board or flat ruler and sharp scissors
- Snap fasteners or hook-and-loop tape

Pattern pieces

You will need the following pattern pieces from pattern sheet ❀. Trace the pieces onto tracing paper and cut them out. A ½in (1cm) seam allowance is included in all pattern pieces. Use a ½in (1cm) seam allowance throughout the pattern, unless otherwise stated.

22 BIB cut 1 in main fabric.
Cut 1 in contrast fabric

23 HEAD cut 1 in contrast fabric.
Cut 1 in interfacing

24 EYE PATCH cut 1 in contrast fabric.
Cut 1 in interfacing

25 NOSE cut 1 in contrast fabric.
Cut 1 in interfacing

26 COLLAR cut 1 in contrast fabric.
Cut 1 in interfacing

27 CHEF'S HAT cut 1 in contrast fabric.
Cut 1 in interfacing

28 EYES cut 2 in black felt.
Cut 2 in interfacing

Baby bibs

Step 1

For the plain bib, place both pieces right side together and pin around the edges A. Machine-stitch around all sides leaving a 1in (2.5cm) opening at the bottom edge for turning. Turn right side out, fold turning seams to wrong side and press.

Step 2

Topstitch around all edges using the sewing machine. Hand-stitch the snap fasteners in place at the neck of bib **B**.

TOP TIP
If you don't want to use snap fasteners as the neck closure you could sew on squares of hook-and-loop tape instead.

Step 3

For the appliqué bib, assemble the template pieces and position them in the centre of the main bib piece, following the numerical order of the template pieces 23–28. Refer also to the placement guide provided on the pattern sheet. When all the pieces are assembled, iron the interfacing to fix in place **C** (see page 134 for more on appliqué).

Step 4

Using contrast thread, work a zigzag stitch around the outer edge of the silhouette. Then, following the template, pick out the hat detail and work around the outer edges of the eye patch, nose and collar in zigzag stitch. Use black thread and a sewing needle to backstitch the felt eyes to the dog's face **D**.

Step 5

Follow steps 1 and 2 to assemble the bib.

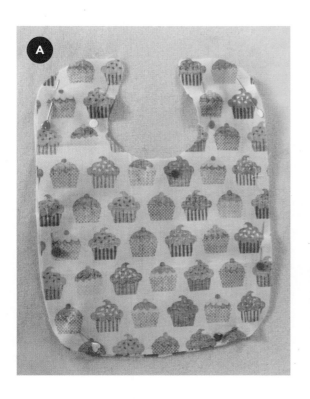

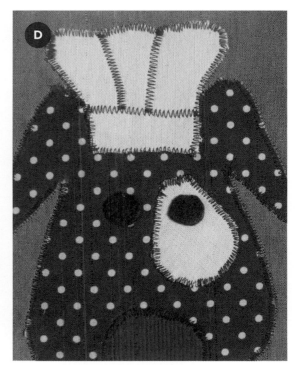

Nursing cushion

This patchwork cushion cover is perfect for using up those odd scraps of leftover fabric that you may have hoarded over the years. It has an envelope fastening to make it easy to slip on and off. I've chosen to back the cushion with soft fleece for comfort and softness at feeding time.

You will need
- 4 fat quarters of contrast fabric
- 60in (152cm) of fleece
- Contrast sewing thread
- Sewing machine
- Hand-sewing needle
- Dressmaking shears
- Pins and pincushion
- Iron and ironing board
- Rotary cutter and board or flat ruler and sharp scissors
- V-shaped cushion pad

Pattern pieces
You will need the following pattern piece from pattern sheet **C**. Trace it onto tracing paper and cut it out. A ½in (1cm) seam allowance is included in all pieces. Use a ½in (1cm) seam allowance throughout the pattern, unless otherwise stated.

29 **CUSHION** cut 2 in patchwork. Cut 1 in fleece. Cut 1 in fleece with 6in (15cm) extension flap

PATCHES Cut 36 squares 5½ x 5½in (14 x 14cm). Cut 9 in each colourway. Assemble mirror images of the patchwork pieces following the diagram below. Then cut the template shape from the top 6 squares of each assembled piece.

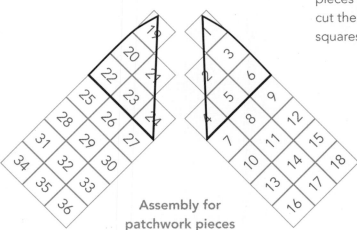

Assembly for patchwork pieces

Nursing cushion

Step 1
Use the layout guide with the template to assemble the patches for both sides (they should mirror each other). Sew together the first row of the first side **A**. Press the seams open at the back of the work.

Step 2
When you have assembled two rows of patches, stitch both rows together. Press the seams open as you go **B**.

Step 3
Continue assembling the rows, stitching to the main body of the fabric until you have completed one side **C**. Use the template to cut out the top of the V.

Step 4
Assemble the patches for the second side, so they are a mirror image of the first side. When you have finished, use the template to cut out a mirror image of the first side.

Step 5
Join the two pieces together along the sloping line at the top of the V **D**. Press the seams open to the back of the work.

Step 6
Neaten then fold up the lower hem at the bottom of one of the sides of the front piece by ½in (1cm). Press and machine-stitch **E**.

Step 7
Cut out the fleece templates, remembering to add a 6in (15cm) extension to the lower half of one of the pieces. Join the two pieces together along the sloping line at the top of the V as you did for the front piece.

Step 8
Lay out the patchwork piece on a flat surface with the right side facing up. Place the fleece piece on to it with wrong side facing up and fold up the extension flap by 6in (15cm) **F** and pin all around.

Step 9
Starting at the inside bottom corner by the extension flap, join the two pieces as follows: machine sew around the inside edge, across the short end and then around the outer edge, leaving an opening beneath the extension flap. Turn right side out and press. Insert the cushion.

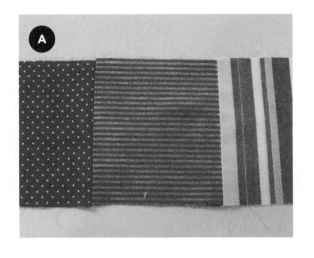

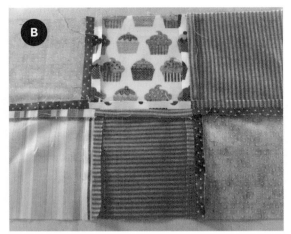

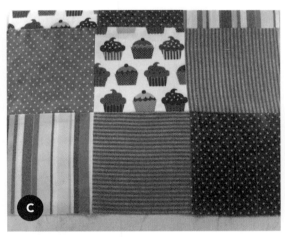

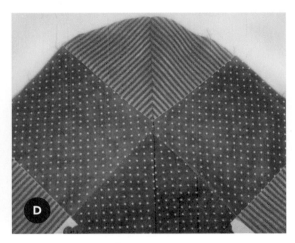

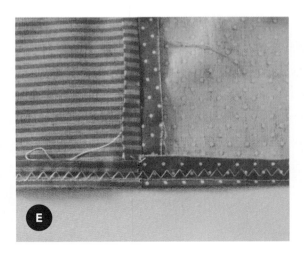

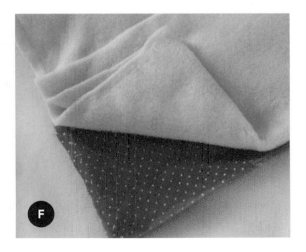

Toys and games

Flower garden cot mobile

This simple toy will keep your baby happy for hours as butterflies and smiley flowers dance and play above the cot. The simple tied attachment means you could also use it on the pram or baby chair too.

You will need

- 2 x fat quarters in contrasting fabrics for each flower/butterfly
- 2 squares of 9 x 9in (23 x 23cm) coloured felt
- Small amount of double-sided fusible interfacing for appliqué
- 3¼yd (3m) of red rickrack ribbon
- Polyester toy filling
- Black embroidery thread
- Contrast sewing thread
- Sewing machine
- Hand-sewing needle
- Dressmaking shears
- Pins and pincushion
- Iron and ironing board

Pattern pieces

You will need the following pattern pieces from pattern sheet **A**. Trace the pieces onto tracing paper and cut them out. A ½in (1cm) seam allowance is included in all pattern pieces. Use a ½in (1cm) seam allowance throughout the pattern, unless otherwise stated.

30 **BUTTERFLY BODY** cut 2 in main fabric. Cut 2 in contrast fabric
31 **BUTTERFLY CENTRE** cut 2 in contrast fabric. Cut 2 in main fabric. Cut 4 in interfacing
32 **PETALS** cut 24 in main fabric
33 **FLOWER CENTRES** cut 4 in felt

Flower garden cot mobile

Step 1
Iron the interfacing to attach a butterfly centre to each butterfly piece. Work a zigzag stitch around the edges of each pad **A** (see page 134 for more on appliqué).

Step 2
Cut a 4in (10cm) piece of rickrack for the hanging loop and fold in half. Pin both pieces of the butterfly together with right sides facing, making sure to sandwich the raw ends of the hanging loop at the top.

Step 3
Machine-stitch around all edges, making sure to leave a 1in (2.5cm) opening for turning. Turn right side out and stuff firmly through the hole **B**. Sew the opening with small, neat slipstitch (see page 136). Repeat for the second butterfly.

Step 4
For the flowers, arrange six pairs of petal pieces with right sides facing. Sew around the curved edges and turn right side out. Stuff firmly through the openings **C**.

Step 5
Cut an 8in (20cm) piece of rickrack for the hanging loop and fold in half. Arrange the petals around one of the felt circles. Place the hanging loop between one of the petals. Pin and tack the petals and loop in place **D**. Machine-stitch to secure.

Step 6
Place the second felt circle on top of first circle with wrong sides facing. Carefully tuck a seam allowance under around the curved edge of this circle and pin in place. Using contrast thread and a hand-sewing needle, stitch around this seam using firm slipstitch. Leave a gap of approximately 1in (2.5cm) from the end and stuff the centre of the flower firmly **E**. Close the opening with small, firm slipstitch.

Step 7
Using black embroidery thread and a hand-sewing needle, work a smiley mouth in backstitch. Then work two French knots for the eyes **F** (see page 136). Repeat steps 4–7 for the second flower.

Step 8
Cut a piece of rickrack long enough to span the width of your child's cot, with enough spare to tie firmly onto each side bar. Thread the butterflies and flowers along the length, position across the cot and secure by tying firmly to the sidebars.

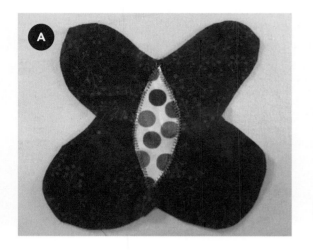

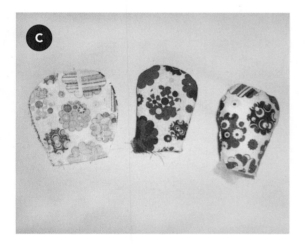

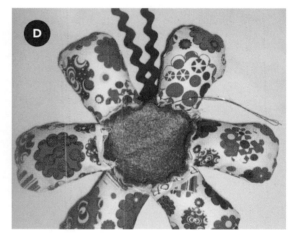

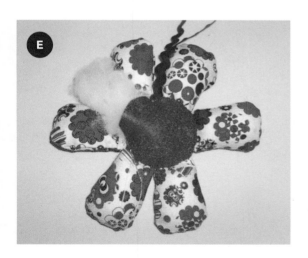

Jack and Daisy rabbit

These cloth toys will make the perfect friends for any child. The limbs and head are made from calico with small scraps of contrast fabric to bring them to life. Choose bright primary colours or pretty prints for a different look.

You will need

- 20in (50cm) calico
- 1 fat quarter contrast fabric for the body
- 1 fat quarter contrast fabric for soles, ear linings and paw pads
- Small amount of double-sided fusible interfacing
- A pair of small toy eyes
- Small piece of pink or blue felt
- 2 small contrast buttons
- Fabric glue
- Small amount of pink ribbon (optional)
- Polyester toy filling
- Contrast thread for hand- and machine-sewing
- Sewing machine
- Hand-sewing needle
- Dressmaking shears
- Pins and pin cushion
- Iron and ironing board
- Fabric marker or tailor's chalk

Pattern pieces

You will need the following pattern pieces from pattern sheet **A**. Trace them onto tracing paper and then cut them out.
A ½in (1cm) seam allowance is included in all pattern pieces. Use a ½in (1cm) seam allowance throughout the pattern, unless otherwise stated.

34 BODY cut 2 in contrast fabric
35 FACE cut 2 in calico
36 HEAD cut 2 in calico
37 EARS cut 4 in calico
38 EAR LININGS cut 2 in contrast fabric. Cut 2 in interfacing
39 ARMS cut 4 in calico
40 PADS cut 2 in contrast fabric. Cut 2 in interfacing
41 LEGS cut 2 in calico
42 SOLES cut 2 in contrast fabric

Jack and Daisy rabbit

Step 1
Attach a paw pad to two of the arm pieces by fusing with a small piece of interfacing. Set your sewing machine to zigzag and stitch around the edge of each paw pad **A** (see page 134 for more on appliqué).

Step 2
With right sides facing, place each arm piece with pad on top of a blank arm piece. Use your sewing machine to work a straight stitch around the edges. Leave a 1¼in (2.5cm) opening along one edge for stuffing. Clip the curves (see page 138) and turn right side out. Stuff firmly. Using a sewing needle and contrast thread, close opening with firm slipstitch **B** (see page 136).

Step 3
Attach ear lining to two of the ear pieces as follows using double-sided fusible interfacing: Attach the lining to the centre of each ear. Work a zigzag stitch around the edge of each lining, as for the paw pads. With right sides facing, place each ear piece with lining on top of a blank ear piece. Sew together with a straight stitch around the edges, leaving a 1¼in (2.5cm) opening along one edge for stuffing. Clip the curves, turn right side out and press. Using a sewing needle and contrast thread, close the openings with firm slipstitch, as for the arms **C**.

Step 4
Fold the leg pieces in half lengthwise. Machine-stitch along the long seam. Position the sole at the bottom of each foot making sure that right sides are together. Pin, tack and then machine-stitch both parts together. Clip the curves. Using a loop turner (see page 131) turn each leg right side out and stuff firmly. I used a knitting needle to help coax the stuffing to the bottom of the legs **D**.

> **TOP TIP**
> You can make a whole family of rabbits by using contrasting fat quarters and adding accessories for each different character.

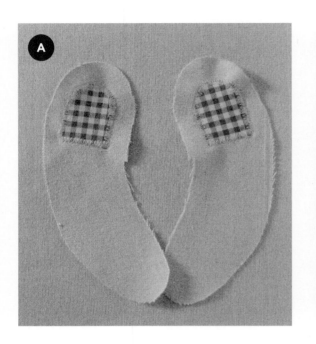

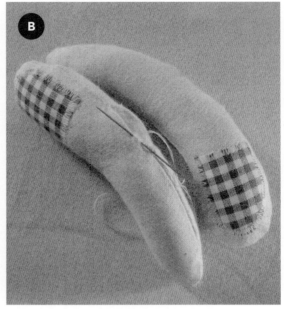

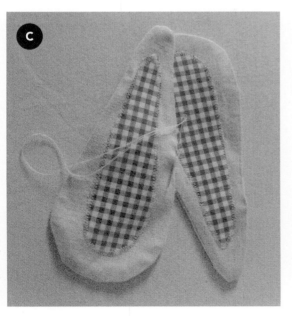

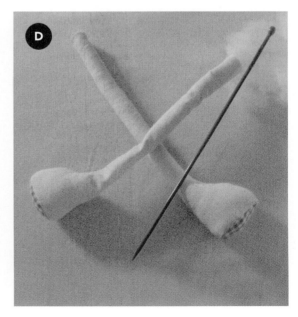

Step 5

Mark the position of the darts on both body pieces using a fabric marker or tailor's chalk. Stitch the dart and press the seam to one side. Place body pieces right sides together, positioning the top of the legs between both layers at the widest part of the body triangle. Point the legs upwards so that they will be in the correct position when you have sewn the sides. Pin and tack the three long sides in place, leaving the neck open for turning **E**. Machine-stitch around the three sides and turn right side out.

Step 6

Stuff the body firmly and, using a sewing needle and contrast thread, close the opening with firm slipstitch **F**.

Step 7

Place the two pieces of the front head right sides together. Machine-stitch along the curved edge. Clip the curves and turn right side out. Repeat for the two back head pieces. Fold the point of each ear in half and position one on either side of the seam line on the back of the head. Pin and tack in place **G**. With right sides facing, place the front of head and back of head together. Match the seam line and make sure the ears do not move. Pin and tack and check you are happy with the ear position. Stitch all layers with the sewing machine. Clip the curves and turn the head right side out.

Step 8

Mark the position of each eye using a fabric marker or tailor's chalk. Snip a small hole in the calico. Fasten the toy eyes securely. Cut a small circle of pink or blue felt and attach to the nose using fabric glue. Stuff the head firmly with toy stuffing. Sew the lower part of the head closed with slipstitch.

Step 9

Hand-sew the head to the body with firm stitches **H**. For Daisy rabbit, cut a small amount of pink ribbon and tie into a bow. Stitch the bow between the ears with a sewing needle and contrast thread.

Step 10

Attach the arms using the jointing method as follows: Pin the arms to the sides of the body at the top. Thread a needle with a long piece of thread and double it for strength. Starting on one arm at the pin position, push the needle all the way through the arm, the body and the arm on the opposite side. Now go back through the body in the opposite direction taking the needle through all the layers and coming out on the first side at the same point. Repeat until the limbs are secure, pulling the thread tightly each time so you get a little dimple where the needle enters and exits the limb. When you are satisfied you have secured the limb properly, fasten off. Sew a button on top of each shoulder to finish.

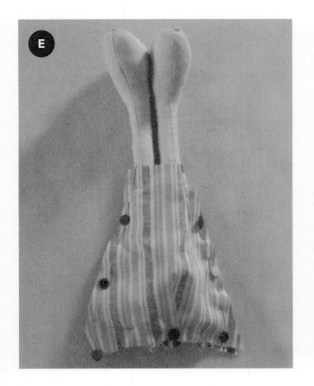

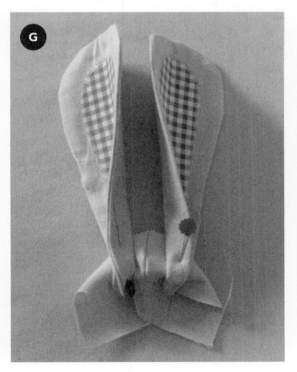

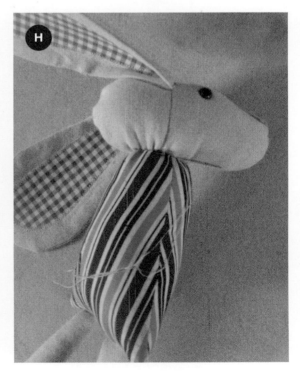

Picnic basket & fruit

All children love pretend play and this soft picnic basket filled with fruit is so easy to make. There is a matching picnic blanket, so the fruit can be spread out just like a real picnic! The handy basket keeps everything together.

You will need

- 20in (50cm) main fabric
- 20in (50cm) of contrast fabric
- 9 x 13in (23 x 33cm) piece of wadding
- 4 fat quarters of contrast fabric
- Polyester toy filling
- Contrast thread
- Sewing machine
- Hand-sewing needle
- Dressmaking shears
- Pins and pincushion
- Iron and ironing board

Pattern pieces

You will need the following pattern pieces from pattern sheet **A**. Trace the pieces onto tracing paper and cut them out. A ½in (1cm) seam allowance is included in all pattern pieces. Use a ½in (1cm) seam allowance throughout the pattern, unless otherwise stated.

43 PEAR cut 2 in contrast fabric
44 APPLE cut 2 in contrast fabric
45 ORANGE cut 2 in contrast fabric
46 BANANA cut 2 in contrast fabric
47 STALK cut 1 in contrast fabric
48 LEAF cut 2 in contrast fabric
PICNIC BASKET 9 x 13in (23 x 33cm)
Cut 1 in main fabric. Cut 1 in contrast fabric.
Cut 1 in batting
STRAPS 2 x 14in (5 x 36cm). Cut 1 in main fabric. Cut 1 in contrast fabric
TABLECLOTH 11 x 14in (28 x 36cm).
Cut 1 in main fabric. Cut 1 in contrast fabric

Picnic basket & fruit

Step 1

To make the picnic basket, pin the batting on top of the wrong side of the main fabric piece. Machine-stitch down each short edge **A**.

Step 2

With right sides facing, fold it in half with the short edges together and machine-stitch down the side seams. You will now have an inside-out bag shape. Machine-stitch across the lower edge of each corner **B**. Snip the excess fabric. Now take the contrast fabric for the lining, and with right sides facing, fold it in half with the short edges together. Pin and machine-stitch the side seams and across the lower edge of each corner, as before. Snip the excess fabric.

Step 3

Place both strap pieces together with right sides facing and machine-stitch down one long edge. Open out and press seam to one side. Press the outer edges in by ⅜in (1cm) on each side **C**.

Step 4

Fold the strap along the sewn seam, with wrong sides facing. Pin and topstitch down each long edge **D**.

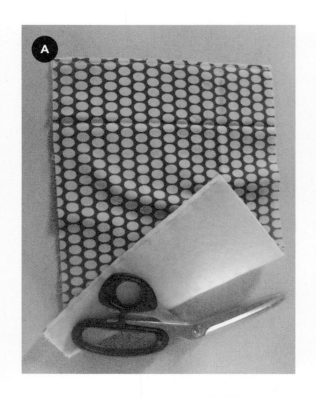

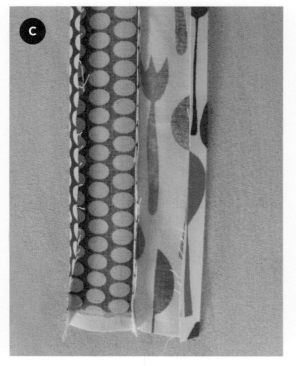

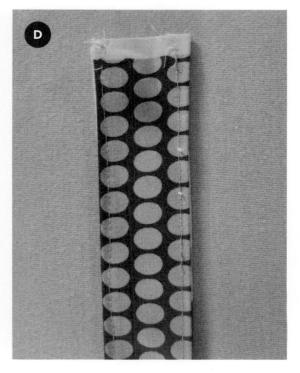

Step 5

Take the inside-out bag and pin the short edges of the strap to the side edges of the bag, right sides together. Then drop the lining into the bag, right sides together, sandwiching the handle in between. Pin in place **E**. Machine-stitch around the top edge, leaving a 1in (2.5cm) opening for turning right side out again.

Step 6

Turn the whole bag right side out, leaving a small edge of lining showing at the top edge of the bag. Tuck under the open seams of the turning hole and topstitch around the top of the bag **F**.

Step 7

With right sides facing, fold the stalk of each piece of fruit in half lengthwise and machine the long edge. Turn right side out and press flat. Fold the stalk in half to make a loop.

Step 8

For the pear, place the main pieces together, right sides facing. Sandwich the raw ends of the stalk at the top **G**. Machine-stitch around all edges, leaving a 1¼in (3cm) opening for turning. Turn right side out and stuff firmly. Close opening with neat, firm slipstitch **H**. Repeat for the banana.

Step 9

Place both pieces of the leaf together with wrong sides facing. Use straight or zigzag stitch and sew around the outer edge approximately ¼in (6mm) from the raw edge. Use neat, firm stitches to sew the leaf to the fruit at the base of the stalk. Repeat steps 8–9 for the apple and orange.

Step 10

For the tablecloth, place both pieces together with right sides facing. Machine-stitch around all the edges leaving a 1¼in (3cm) opening for turning. Turn right side out and press. Tuck under the raw edges of the opening. Topstitch around all the edges.

TOP TIP
You can use scraps of leftover fabric to make these soft fruits. Who says a banana has to be yellow?

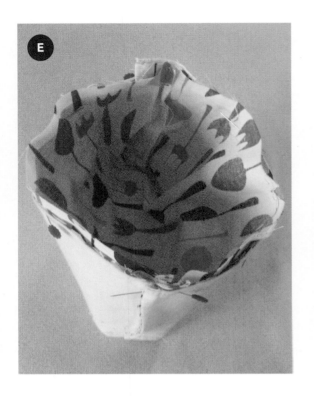

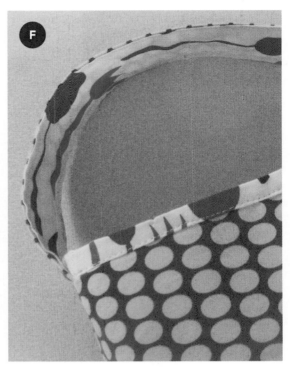

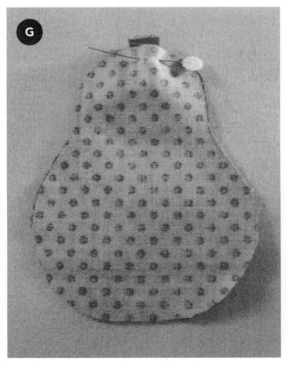

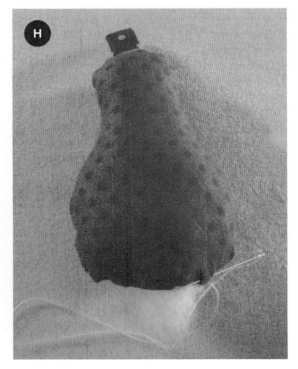

Sunshine skittles

This ball-and-skittles game is great for developing your toddler's hand and eye co-ordination. The bright numbers on the front also make for a fun way to practise counting.

You will need

- 8 fat quarters of brightly coloured fabric
- 9 x 9in (23 x 23cm), 1 yellow and 1 orange
- Small bell for the centre of the ball (optional)
- Fabric glue
- Polyester toy filling
- Contrast sewing thread
- Sewing machine
- Hand-sewing needle
- Dressmaking shears
- Pins and pincushion
- Iron and ironing board

Pattern pieces

You will need the following pattern pieces from pattern sheet **C**. Trace the pieces onto tracing paper and cut them out. A ½in (1cm) seam allowance is included in all pattern pieces. Use a ½in (1cm) seam allowance throughout the pattern, unless otherwise stated.

49 BALL cut 8 (2 in each contrast fabric)
50 SKITTLE BODY cut 4 (1 in each contrast fabric)
51 SKITTLE BASE cut 1 in contrast fabric
52 – **57** NUMBERS cut 1 each in felt

Sunshine skittles

Step 1
Arrange the ball pieces into four sets of pairs
A. Pin the pieces of each pair, right sides
together, aligning edges and points.

Step 2
Machine-stitch down the long edge of each
pair. Work from point to point, making sure
to follow the curves. Open the pairs out and
press, with the seams to one side **B**. Pin two
sewn pieces together, right sides facing and
align the edges. Sew down the long edge of
each set and press leaving two half spheres.

Step 3
Pin the two sewn pieces together, right sides
facing, and align the cut edges. Sew down
the long edge of each set of pieces, working
from point to point. Press. You will have two
half spheres. Turn one half sphere right side
out and tuck it inside the other half sphere so
the right sides are facing together. Line up all
cut edges and pin pieces together. Machine-
stitch around the seam, beginning about 1¼in
(3cm) in from the top point. Leave this open
for stuffing. Stuff firmly, inserting the bell
(optional). Slipstitch to close the opening **C**.

Step 4
Pin the long skittle pieces in two pairs, right
sides together, carefully aligning edges and

points. Machine-stitch one long side of each
pair, working from point to point, making sure
to follow the curves.

Step 5
Open the pairs out and press. Press the
seams to one side **D**. Turn one pair right side
out and tuck it inside the other pair so the
right sides are facing together. Line up all cut
edges and pin the pieces together.

Step 6
Starting at the top point, machine-stitch down
one long edge. Then machine-stitch down
the second long edge, leaving a 1¼in (3cm)
opening along this side for stuffing.

Step 7
With right sides facing, pin the base to the
bottom of the skittle. Machine-stitch round
the whole edge. Turn skittle right side out
through the side opening and stuff firmly **E**.
Close the opening with neat slipstitch.

Step 8
Attach a felt number to each skittle using
fabric glue. To make the numbers even more
secure, topstitch by hand, using a contrast
thread and small, neat running stitch **F**.

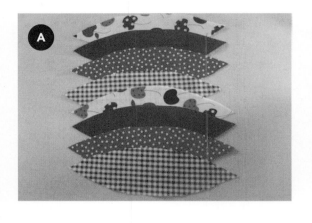

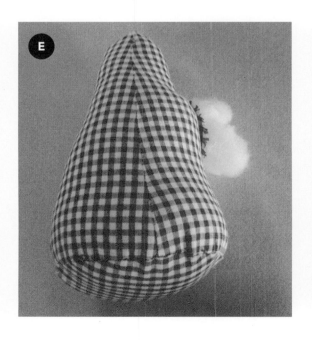

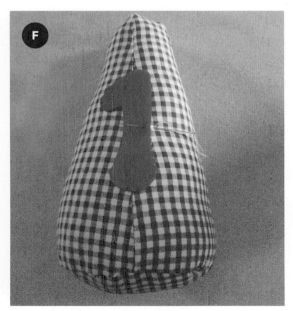

Elephant cot toy

This sleepy elephant will help keep your baby company at bedtime. With bright contrast fabrics and a beaded tail for little hands to squeeze and explore, you might even manage a lie-in yourself!

You will need

- 20in (50cm) of turquoise linen or cotton fabric
- 1 fat quarter of contrast fabric
- A handful of brightly coloured beads
- Red embroidery thread
- 1 small button
- 1 snap fastener
- Polyester toy filling
- Small amount of double-sided fusible interfacing for appliqué
- Contrast sewing thread
- Sewing machine
- Hand-sewing needle
- Dressmaking shears
- Pins and pincushion
- Iron and ironing board
- Loop turner

Pattern pieces

You will need the following pattern pieces from pattern sheet **B**. Trace the pieces onto tracing paper and cut them out. A ½in (1cm) seam allowance is included in all pattern pieces. Use a ½in (1cm) seam allowance throughout the pattern, unless otherwise stated.

Remember to cut mirror images of the body and ears (see page 129 for more on laying and cutting out fabric).

58 **BODY** cut 2 in main fabric
59 **EARS** cut 2 in main fabric. Cut 2 in contrast fabric
60 **SEAT** cut 2 in contrast fabric. Cut 2 in interfacing
STRAP cut 2 x 17in (5 x 43cm) length in contrast fabric

Elephant cot toy

Step 1
Attach the seat to the back of each main body piece with your iron to fuse the interfacing. Set your sewing machine to zigzag and stitch around the lower curved edges of each seat **A** (see page 134 for more on appliqué).

Step 2
Place two ear pieces together in contrasting fabrics, right sides facing. Pin and machine-stitch around all curved edges **B**. Turn right side out and press. Repeat for the other ear.

Step 3
Using the marks noted on the pattern, position one ear on the right side of one elephant body piece **C**. Machine-stitch in place. Repeat for the other ear.

Step 4
Using red embroidery thread, make a twisted cord or plait approximately 5in (13cm) long and knot one end. Thread an assortment of coloured beads onto the tail and knot the opposite end to prevent the beads sliding off **D**.

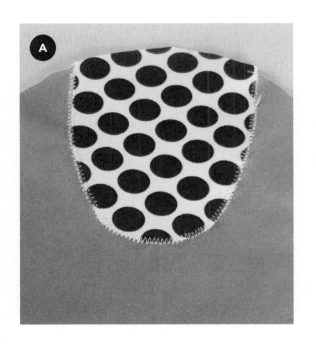

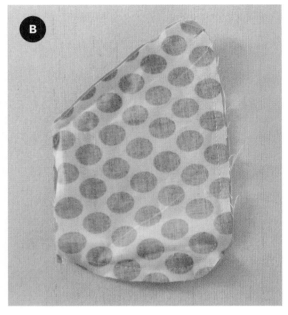

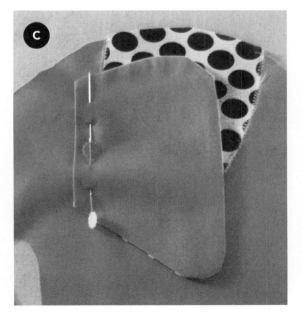

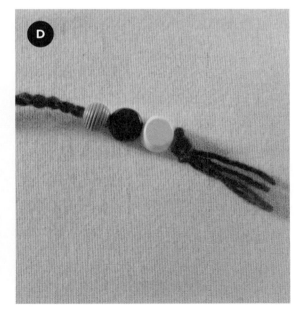

Step 5

Place the two pieces of the hanging loop
together with right sides facing. Sew around
both long edges and one short edge. Use
a loop turner to turn the loop right side out
E (see page 131).

Step 6

Place the main body pieces of the elephant
together with right sides facing. Slide the tail
into place, making sure you have enclosed
one end firmly within the sandwich. Position
the hanging loop at the top of the elephant,
in the middle of seat and pin the raw
edge firmly within the seam **F**.

Step 7

Machine-stitch around all edges, leaving
a 1in (2.5cm) opening just below the tail for
turning. Turn right side out and stuff firmly.
Close the opening using contrast thread
and neat slipstitch **G**.

Step 8

Use the hanging loop to position the
elephant on the bars of the cot by folding
the hanger over the top bar. When you
are happy with the height, mark the position
onto the hanging loop. Sew a snap fastener
on the loop in the position you have marked.
Sew a decorative button on top.

Step 9

Transfer the eye motif to the main body
of the elephant (see page 128 on transferring
patterns). Using embroidery thread, embroider
the elephant's eye and lashes with backstitch
H (see page 136).

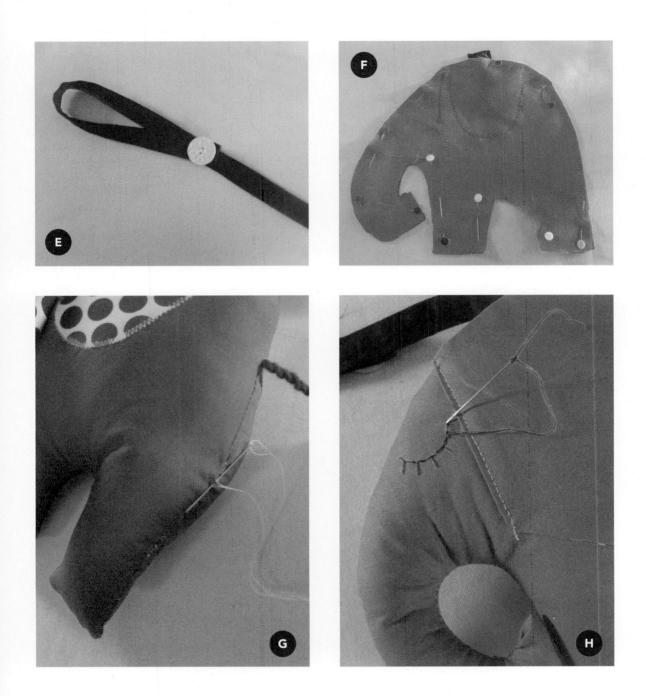

Clothes and shoes

Tulip dungarees

These versatile dungarees can be made in a range of fabrics. Use denim, cotton florals or replace the pockets with a contrasting spot or stripe material if you prefer. The legs fasten with poppers for easy access at changing time.

You will need
- 20in (50cm) denim or cotton fabric
- 20in (50cm) contrast fabric
- Small pieces of contrast fabric for appliqué
- Small amount of double-sided fusible interfacing
- 20in (50cm) of ⅛in (3mm) ribbon
- 2 buttons
- 5 snap fasteners
- Contrast sewing thread
- Embroidery thread
- Sewing machine
- Hand-sewing needle
- Dressmaking shears
- Pins and pincushion
- Iron and ironing board

Sizes
To fit 0–6 months [6–12 months: 1–2 years]
Size shown on model: 6–12 months

Pattern pieces
You will need the following pattern pieces from pattern sheets **D** and **E**. Trace the pieces onto tracing paper and cut them out. A ⅝in (1.5cm) seam allowance is included in all pattern pieces. Use a ⅝in (1.5cm) seam allowance throughout, unless otherwise stated.

61 BACK cut 2 in main fabric
62 FRONT cut 2 in main fabric
63 BACK FACING cut 1 in contrast fabric. Cut 1 in interfacing
64 FRONT FACING cut 1 in contrast fabric. Cut 1 in interfacing
65 POCKETS cut 3 in main fabric
66 LEG CUFFS cut 2 in main fabric
67 TULIP APPLIQUÉ cut 3 in contrast fabric. Cut 3 in interfacing
LEG FACINGS 2 x 16[17:18]in (5 x 41[43:45]cm) cut 2 in contrast fabric

Tulip dungarees

Step 1

The pattern features three pockets with an appliqué motif (see page 134 for appliqué techniques). I made the tulip heads in yellow fabric and the leaves in green. Cut three of each in your chosen fabric and double-sided fusible interfacing.

Step 2

Position the motif onto each pocket, placing the leaf first, with the flower on top of it. When all the pieces are assembled, iron to attach the interfacing **A**. Work a zigzag stitch around the outer edge of the silhouette and across the leaves and flower head, following the template lines **B**.

Step 3

Press under ¼in (6mm) on top edge of pocket. Turn the top edge to outside along the fold line to form a facing. Stitch along the seam line around the raw edge **C**.

Step 4

Trim bulk and turn facing right side out. Tuck seam allowance to wrong side around lower edges and press **D**. Follow steps 2–4 for the other two pockets.

Step 5

Take the front two sections for the dungarees. Work a zigzag stitch down each centre front edge to neaten. Pin and tack the pieces right sides together, then machine-stitch the seam. Clip the curves (see page 138) and press the seam open **E**. Pin and tack the pocket to the front, then topstitch in place **F**.

TOP TIP
If using denim for your dungarees, always wash before cutting out your pieces to pre-empt any shrinkage or colour run.

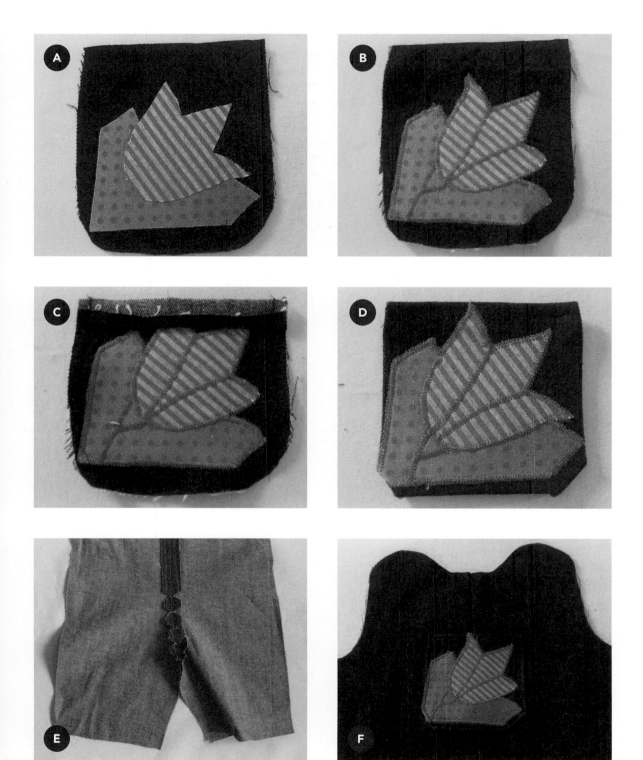

Step 6

Take the back two sections and work a zigzag stitch down each centre-back edge to neaten. Pin the right sides together and machine-stitch the seam, clip the curves and press open **G**. Pin and tack the remaining two pockets onto the seat of the back. See photo above right for reference when placing them. Topstitch in place.

Step 7

Neaten the side edges of front and back pieces with zigzag stitch. Place the front and back sections right sides together, pin the side seams and machine-stitch. Press the seams open **H**.

Step 8

Iron the fusible interfacing to the wrong sides of back and front facing. Fold ¼in (6mm) of the lower edge to the wrong side and secure with zigzag stitch **I**.

Step 9

Pin and sew the side seams of the back and front facings. With the right sides facing, pin the facing to the dungarees around the neck, shoulders and armholes **J**. The dungarees should be sandwiched between the facing. Machine-stitch around the neck, shoulder and armhole edges. Trim the seam and clip the curves. Turn the facing to inside and press. If you like, you can now topstitch in a contrast colour around the neck, shoulder and armhole edges (optional).

Step 10

Sew a snap fastener on the facing side of each back strap. Sew the corresponding piece of the snap fastener to the front of the dungarees. Sew a button on the right side of each back strap for decoration.

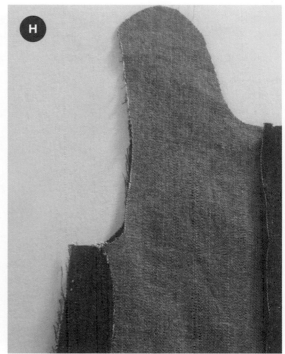

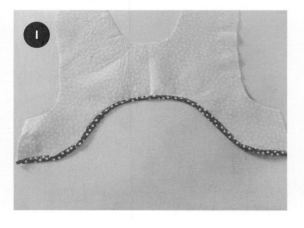

Step 11

For the lower cuffs, hand-sew a line of gathering stitches along the lower edge of both legs. Draw up the fabric until it matches the length of the cuff piece **K**. With right sides facing, pin the cuff to the lower edge **L**. Machine-stitch the seam and press.

Step 12

Fold the cuff in half lengthways and press, then open it out **M**. Cut the length of ribbon in half and pin one piece in place along the upper half of the cuff. Topstitch in place. Repeat for the second leg.

Step 13

Fold the cuff along the pressed line to the inside of the leg. Press a ¼in (6mm) seam allowance under at the raw edge and slipstitch the cuff along the stitching line on the wrong side.

Step 14

Take the leg facing and press a ¼in (6mm) seam allowance along one long edge and at each end. With right sides together, place front leg facing on the front of the legs. Pin the raw edge in place using a ³⁄₈in (1cm) seam allowance **N**. Machine-stitch the seam.

Step 15

Turn right-side out so the facing is on the inside. Press and pin the facing in place **O**. Slipstitch the turned edge and topstitch the outside seam edge.

Step 16

Starting on the front of the legs, position one snap fastener on the facing at the crotch, on each cuff and on either side between crotch and cuff. Hand-stitch them firmly in place. Repeat for the back of legs, stitching the corresponding part of the fastener to the denim side **P**.

Japanese doll sundress

I have designed this simple little sundress with beginners in mind. There are no tricky facings or buttonholes to wrestle with and by using ready-made bias binding you could realistically whip up this cute number in a day.

You will need
- 40in (1m) of main fabric
- Small pieces contrast fabric, black, red and pink felt for the appliqué
- Double-sided fusible interfacing
- 20in (50cm) of ³⁄₁₆in (5mm) elastic
- 3¾yd (3.5m) red bias binding
- Black and red embroidery thread
- Black thread and contrast sewing thread
- Sewing machine
- Hand-sewing needle
- Dressmaking shears
- Pins and pincushion
- Iron and ironing board

Sizes
To fit 3–9 months [9–12 months: 1–2 years: 2–3 years]
Size shown on model: 2–3 years

Pattern pieces
You will need the following pattern pieces from pattern sheet **B**. Trace the pieces onto tracing paper and cut them out.
A ½in (1cm) seam allowance is included in all pattern pieces except the front and back pieces where a 1³⁄₁₆in (3cm) hem allowance has been included and the appliqué pieces. Use a ½in (1cm) seam allowance throughout the pattern, unless otherwise stated.

68 FRONT cut 1 in main fabric
69 BACK cut 1 in main fabric
70 KIMONO cut 1 in contrast fabric. Cut 1 in interfacing
71 FACE cut 1 in pink felt. Cut 1 in interfacing
72 OBI cut 1 in main fabric. Cut 1 in interfacing
73 HAIR cut 1 in black felt. Cut 1 in interfacing
74 FLOWER cut 1 in red felt. Cut 1 in interfacing

Japanese doll sundress

Step 1

Measure 4in (10cm) from the bottom edge of the dress (excluding the hem) and position the doll motif onto the dress following the numerical order of template pieces 70–74. Refer also to the placement guide provided on the pattern sheet. When all the pieces are assembled **A**, iron to attach the interfacing.

Step 2

Using black thread, work a zigzag stitch around the edges and across the obi. Follow the template to work the criss-cross of the neck and sleeves. Use straight stitch to work the inside edge of the hairline and chin **B**. Using black embroidery thread, work two small stitches for eyes. Using red embroidery thread, work a cross for each cheek. Position the flower on the hair and use small stitches to secure **C**.

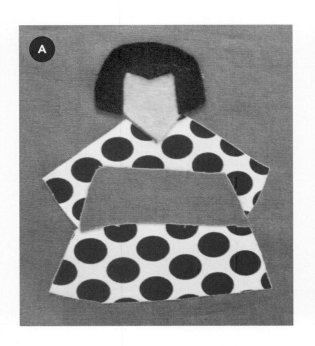

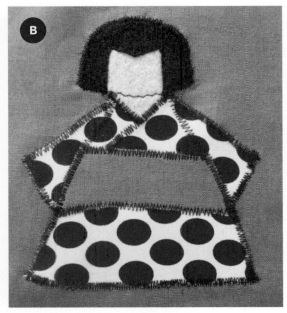

TOP TIP
If you find appliqué tricky, why not try using a ready-made motif to sew on the front of the dress instead? Alternatively, you could choose stripes or floral fabric and add a pocket for detail.

Step 4

Cut a piece of bias binding the same length as the top edge of the front piece. Fold it in half lengthways over the raw edge of the front. Pin and topstitch in place **F**.

Step 5

Cut two lengths of bias binding that are 15[16:17:18]in (38[41:43:46]cm). Beginning at the underarm, fold and pin the binding along the raw edge of the front side curve. Pin in place and topstitch, continuing along the whole length of the bias binding. Repeat for the second side **G**.

Step 6

Sew the side seams and press open .

Step 7

Cut a 30[32:34:36]in (76[81:86:91]cm) length of bias binding. Fold in half lengthways, press and topstitch. Fold this in half and position the middle point at the centre back of the sundress on the wrong side. Machine-stitch in place along the seam line **I**.

Step 3

Work a line of zigzag stitch along the side edges and the hem of the back piece. Fold down the top edge by ½in (1cm) and then again by ½in (1cm). Press, pin and machine-stitch. Thread a length of elastic through, using a safety pin for ease **D**. Machine-stitch across one end of the elastic, then draw the elastic up, ruching the fabric as you go. Secure in place by machine-stitching across the other end of the elastic. Snip the excess **E**.

Step 8

Fold up the hem allowance, pin and press. Hand-sew the hem using neat slipstitch (see page 136 for more on slipstitch).

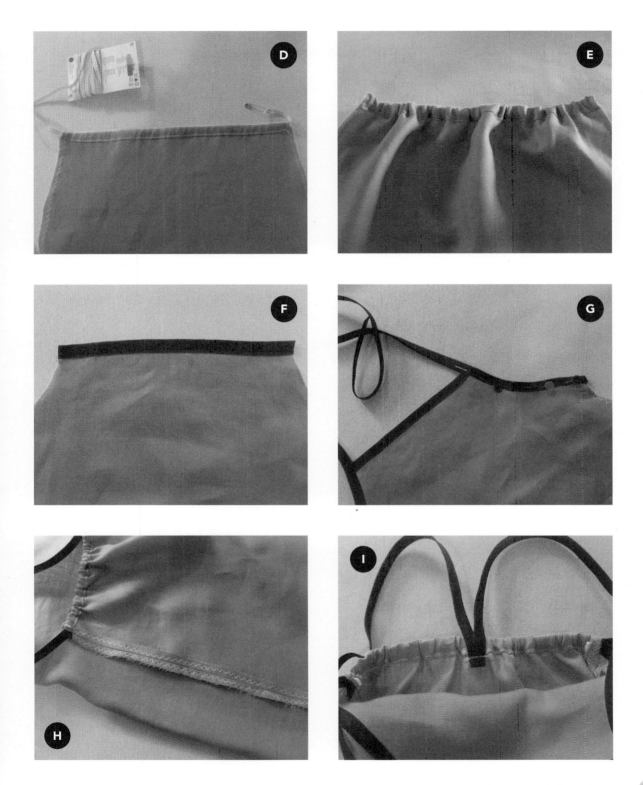

Baby shoes

These adorable shoes are quick and simple to put together and can be made in classic Mary-Jane or ballet style. Why not design your own upper using bright fabrics, appliqué and hand embroidery?

You will need
- 20in (50cm) main fabric
- 20in (50cm) calico
- Small pieces of purple, pale pink and fuchsia felt
- 20in (50cm) length of ¼in (6mm) ribbon for the ballet shoes
- 40in (1m) length of ⅛in (3mm) ribbon for the ballet shoes
- Small amount of ³⁄₁₆in (5mm) elastic for the Mary-Jane shoes
- 2 decorative buttons for the Mary-Jane shoes
- Matching embroidery thread
- Contrast sewing thread
- Sewing machine
- Hand-sewing needle
- Dressmaking shears
- Pins and pincushion
- Iron and ironing board

Sizes
0–6 months [6–9 months]
Size shown on model: 6–9 months

Pattern pieces
You will need the following pattern pieces from pattern sheet **E**. Trace the pieces onto tracing paper and cut them out. A ¼in (6mm) seam allowance is included in all pattern pieces. Use a ¼in (6mm) seam allowance throughout, unless otherwise stated.

Remember to cut mirror images of the soles so you have a left foot and a right foot (see page 129 for more information on laying out and cutting fabric). Transfer the upper template into the middle of the fabric, making sure to follow the grainline so the upper is cut on the bias.

75 SOLES cut 2 in main fabric. Cut 2 in lining fabric
76 UPPER cut 2 in main fabric. Cut 2 in lining fabric
77 SPOTS cut 15 in felt
MARY-JANE STRAP cut 2 pieces 3 x 4in (8 x 10cm) in contrast fabric

Baby shoes

Step 1

Arrange the felt spots inside the outline of the first upper. I used two fuchsia spots, three pale pink spots and two-and-a-half purple spots. Pin in place, then use embroidery thread to run a circle of backstitch around the edge of each spot to secure Ⓐ. Repeat for the second upper.

Step 2

Make sure you have a matching pair – a right and a left foot – before stitching. With right sides together, fold each upper to match at back seam. Pin and machine-stitch this seam, then press open. With right sides together, pin the sole to the upper and machine-stitch. Turn right side out Ⓑ.

Step 3

Again, make sure you have a matching pair before stitching. Fold each lining upper together to match at back seam. Pin and machine-stitch the seam, then press it open. Pin the lining sole to the lining upper, wrong sides together, and machine-stitch. This time, don't turn inside out. Place a lining inside each upper, with wrong sides facing.

Step 4

For the ballet shoes, cut 10 pieces of the ¼in (6mm) ribbon into 2in (5cm) lengths to form the loops. Tuck in the seam allowance around the top edge of the upper shoe and the lining and pin in place. Fold each ribbon loop in half and position around the edges, sandwiching between the upper and lining. Pin two at the front, one on each side and one at the back Ⓒ. Tack the seam and then use your sewing machine to topstitch close to the upper edge. Cut the length of ⅛in (3mm) ribbon in half and thread each piece through the loops to form the ties.

Step 5

For the Mary-Jane shoes, cut the fabric straps in half lengthways, right sides together. Pin and machine-stitch along the long edge. Use a loop turner to turn right side out (see page 131) and press. Thread elastic through strap and stitch the elastic along one short edge. Ruche the fabric down the length of the elastic Ⓓ. Stretch the elastic slightly so it measures 2in (5cm), then pin and stitch the layers. Snip excess fabric and elastic.

Step 6

Tuck in the seam allowance around the top edge of the upper shoe and the lining and pin in place. Sandwich the ends of the strap between the layers and pin Ⓔ. Slipstitch around the top edge of the shoe, making sure to secure the strap ends firmly. Sew a button to the outside of each shoe.

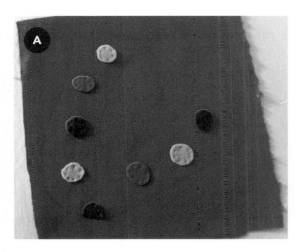

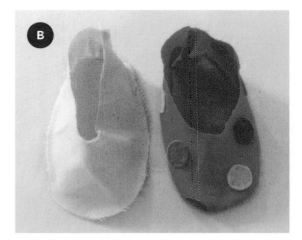

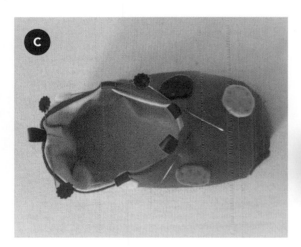

Toddler trousers

These cute trousers are perfect for kids on the move. Designed with plenty of ease and a forgiving, elasticized waist, your little one will be able to crawl, run and climb all day in them. Personalize the contrast details with florals, checks, spots or stripes to your own taste and style.

You will need

- 20in (50cm) corduroy, denim or medium-weight dress fabric
- 10in (25cm) contrast fabric
- 1 fat quarter of contrast fabric
- 4 contrast buttons
- 20in (50cm) of ½in (1cm) elastic
- Contrast sewing thread
- Sewing machine
- Hand-sewing needle
- Dressmaking shears
- Pins and pincushion
- Iron and ironing board

Sizes

To fit 6–12 months [1–2 years: 2–3 years]
Size shown on model: 2–3 years

Pattern pieces

You will need the following pattern pieces from pattern sheet **E**. Trace the pieces onto tracing paper and cut them out. A ⅝in (1.5cm) seam allowance is included in all pattern pieces. Use a ⅝in (1.5cm) seam allowance throughout the pattern, unless otherwise stated.

78 TROUSER FRONT cut 2 in main fabric
79 TROUSER BACK cut 2 in main fabric
80 TROUSER POCKET cut 2 in main fabric
HEM STRAP 2 x 6½in (5 x 17cm)
Cut 4 in main fabric
WAISTBAND CASING 2in x 13[13½:14]in (5 x 36[34:33]cm). Cut 1 in contrast fabric
LOWER HEM 4½ x 14[14½:15]in (11 x 38[37:36]cm). Cut 2 in contrast fabric
POCKET TOP 2 x 3½in (5 x 9cm). Cut 2 in contrast fabric

Toddler trousers

Step 1
Finish the raw edges on each leg piece with zigzag stitching. Pin a front leg and back leg together, right sides facing. Machine-stitch the inside leg seam first, then the outside leg seam . Repeat for the other leg. Press the seams open. With right sides together, place one leg inside the other. Pin and stitch the gusset seam. Clip the curve (see page 138) and press the seam to one side.

Step 2
Fold and press the seam allowance at each end of the waistband casing. With right sides together, pin the casing to the top edge of the trousers . Machine-stitch around the seam and press the seam towards the top. Fold casing to the wrong side of trousers. Press under the seam allowance along the raw edge of the casing. Pin in place then stitch, leaving a 1in (2.5cm) opening at the back seam for threading the elastic through later.

Step 3
Fold one contrast hem in half, right sides facing. Pin and machine-stitch the short edge and press the seam open. Repeat for the second hem piece. Turn the trousers inside out and pin the right side of the lining to the wrong side of the first leg . Machine-stitch around the edge.

Step 4
Turn the trousers right side out. Open out the hem and press the seam. Fold up the seam allowance on the raw edge . Fold the hem in half to meet the bottom edge of the leg and pin . Using contrast thread, slipstitch to secure (see page 136).

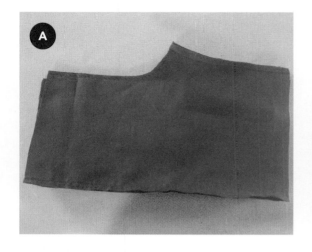

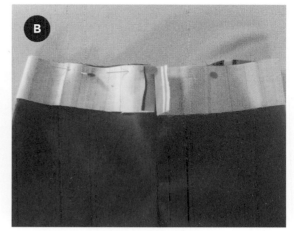

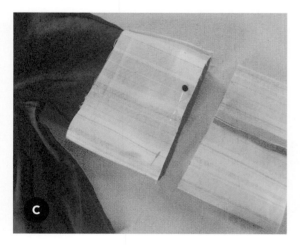

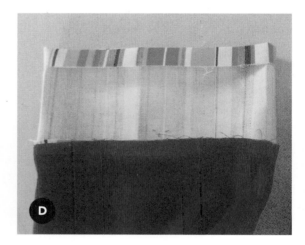

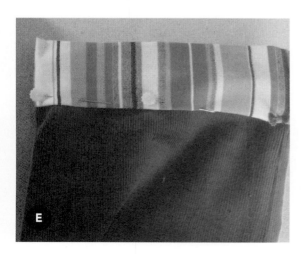

Step 7

With right sides facing, pin and machine-stitch the pocket top to the top of each pocket piece G. Press the seam towards the top. Fold the pocket top in half over the raw edge and press H. Topstitch the pocket top edging to secure in place. Press the seam allowance on each pocket to the wrong side of the fabric. Position the first pocket on outer side of the first leg. Pin and tack in place I. Topstitch around side and bottom edges.

Step 8

Attach a large safety pin to one end of the elastic and use the head of the safety pin to feed the elastic through the waistband casing J. Pull through and adjust the waist size to fit your child. Trim the excess. Stitch the ends of the elastic very firmly, either on the machine or by hand. Sew the opening with neat slipstitch.

Step 5

With right sides facing, pin the two strap pieces together. Machine-stitch the long edges and one short edge. Turn right side out through the other short edge. Topstitch around all the sewn edges.

Step 6

Turn the trousers the wrong side out. Pin the raw edge of one of the hem straps across the hem seam with the main part of the strap facing upwards towards the waistband F. Machine-stitch along the hem seam. Fold the strap to the right side of the trousers and hand-stitch to the side seam with a button for decoration. Repeat for the second leg.

TOP TIP
If you would prefer to make shorts instead of trousers, simply adjust the leg pieces to the required length.

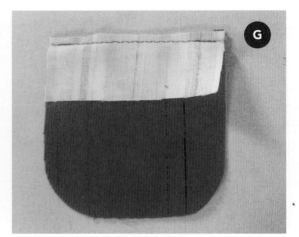

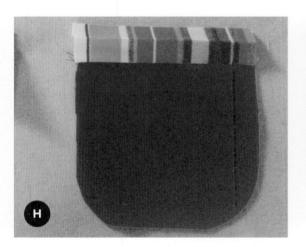

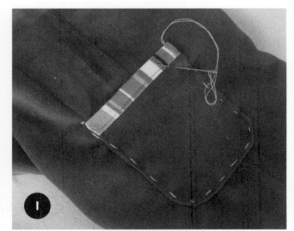

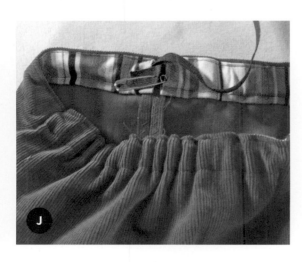

Military shirt

I have designed this shirt with snap closures instead of buttonholes because little fingers find buttons difficult to use. If you are new to dressmaking, there are plenty of other techniques to learn on this project, such as fixing collars and setting in sleeves. You could also make this shirt in floral fabric with rickrack or lace on the sleeves and hem.

You will need
- 20in (50cm) main fabric
- Small pieces contrast material for the stars
- 20in (50cm) double-sided fusible interfacing
- 5 buttons
- 5 chunky snap fasteners
- Embroidery thread for the appliqué
- Contrast sewing thread
- Sewing machine
- Hand-sewing needle
- Dressmaking shears
- Pins and pincushion
- Iron and ironing board

Sizes
To fit 6–12 months [1–2 years: 2–3 years]
Size shown on model: 2–3 years

Pattern pieces
You will need the following pattern pieces from pattern sheet **F**. Trace the pieces onto tracing paper and cut them out. A ⅝in (1.5cm) seam allowance is included in all pattern pieces. Use a ⅝in (1.5cm) seam allowance throughout the pattern, unless otherwise stated.

81 FRONT cut 2 in main fabric
82 SLEEVES cut 2 in main fabric
83 BACK cut 1 in main fabric
84 COLLAR cut 2 in main fabric.
Cut 1 in interfacing
85 POCKET cut 1 in main fabric
86 POCKET FLAP cut 1 in main fabric
87 STARS cut 3 in contrast fabric

Military shirt

Step 1
Stay stitch the front and back neck edges approximately ½in (1cm) away from the cut edge **A**. Stay stitching is used to strengthen curved edges, preventing them from stretching. Turn front facing to wrong side along first fold line and press. Turn over again along second fold line and press. Then turn the facing to outside at neck edge. Pin and machine-stitch neck edge to the dot. Clip down to dot. Turn facing to inside and press again.

Step 2
Press a ¼in (6mm) seam on upper edge of pocket. Turn upper edge to outside and fold down along fold line. Using a ⅝in (1.5cm) seam allowance and starting at the top of the pocket at fold edge, machine-stitch around all three raw edges. Turn the top facing to inside and press raw edges. Position the pocket onto the breast on the left side of the shirt. Pin, tack and topstitch in place **B**.

Step 3
Fold top flap of pocket in half lengthwise with right sides together. Pin and stitch the short edges using a ⅝in (1.5cm) seam allowance. Turn flap right side out and topstitch around the three sides, leaving out the cut edges. Press the raw edge to the wrong side. With right sides facing, pin and tack top flap above the pocket. Topstitch the top edge of flap to

secure. Sew a red button to the centre of the top flap **C**. Sew one part of the snap fastener to the underside of the button. Sew the corresponding fastener to the pocket top.

Step 4
Using the double-sided fusible interfacing, position the stars onto the right breast of the shirt, lining them up with the pocket on the left side. Iron to bond in place, then machine-stitch around all the edges **D**. A little fraying will naturally add to the shirt design.

Step 5
Work zigzag stitch around the shoulder and side seams of front and back pieces to neaten. Pin the front and back pieces, right sides together and machine-stitch the shoulder and side seams. Press seams open **E**.

Step 6
Iron the fusible interfacing to the wrong side of one of the collar pieces. Machine-stitch ⅝in (1.5cm) in from raw edge along the length of the curved edge. Press this seam under and trim to ¼in (6mm). With right sides facing, place both collar pieces together. Using a ⅝in (1.5cm) seam allowance, machine-stitch all three sides, excluding the curved edges. Cut diagonally across the lower corners and trim seam allowances to remove bulk **F**.

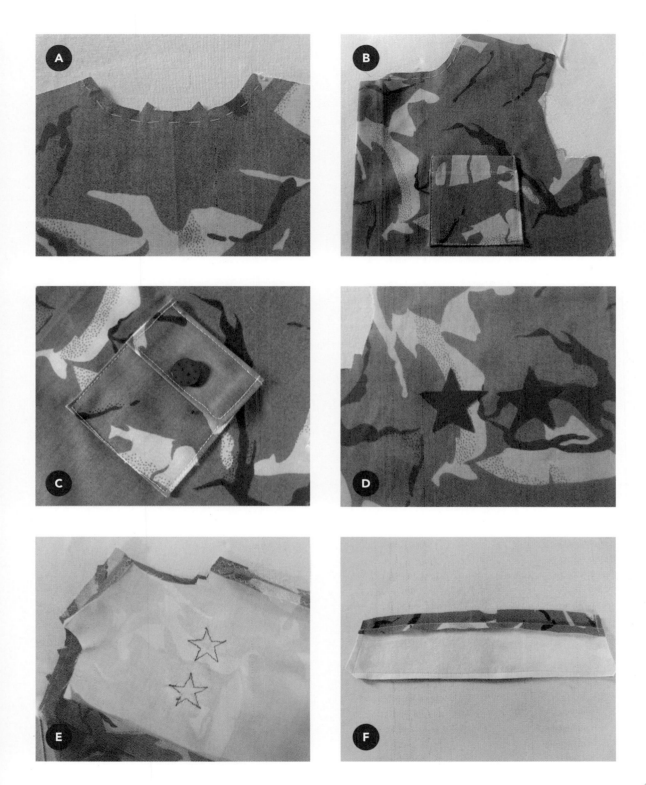

TOP TIP
When making a shirt
where accuracy is important,
always press after every step
and tack where you can.

Step 8

Work zigzag stitch around all sleeve edges to neaten. Appliqué a red star to the centre of one of the sleeves. Run a line of hand-gathering stitches across the sleeve head **I** (see page 135). Using a ⅝in (1.5cm) seam allowance machine-stitch the underarm seam and press open. Press the hem to wrong side. Pin, tack and machine-stitch the hem **J**.

Step 9

Turn sleeve right side out. Hold the garment wrong side out with the armhole facing towards you. With right sides together, pin and tack the sleeve to the armhole edge, matching underarm seams and using the gathering thread to distribute any fullness in the sleeve head evenly **K**. Machine-stitch the seam, clip curves and trim the excess fabric.

Step 7

Turn right side out and press. Clip the neck edge of the shirt to the stay stitching. With right sides facing, pin the collar to the outside edge of shirt along raw (not pressed) edge of the collar, matching seams **G**. Tack and machine-stitch. Trim and clip the curves (see page 138). Pin the pressed edge of collar to inside of shirt **H**. Tack and machine-stitch close to inner pressed edge. Topstitch around finished edges of collar.

Step 10

Topstitch the front edges. Turn up the hem by ¼in (6mm), then again by 1in (2.5cm) and press. Clip any bulk away from the facings. Pin, tack and machine-stitch the hem **L**. Position the buttons along the left front edge and stitch in place. Sew a snap fastener to the underside of each button. Sew a corresponding fastener to the right front edge.

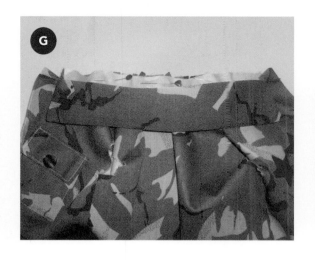

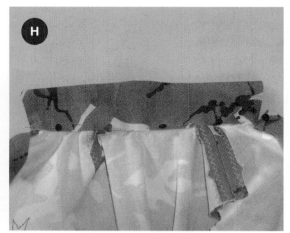

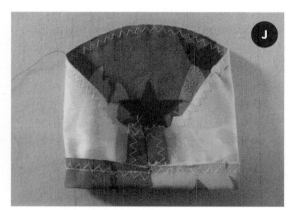

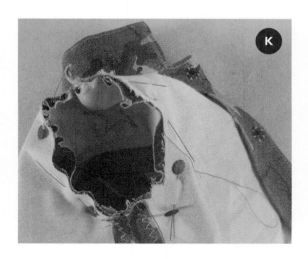

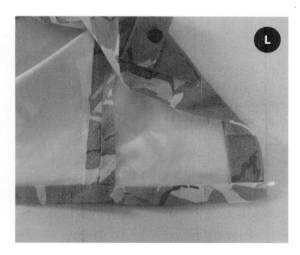

Sewing basics

Patterns & templates

How to use the pattern sheets

All the pattern and template pieces you will need can be found on the pull-out sheets labelled A–F at the back of the book. They are all printed full-size and ready to use. Each pattern piece has a unique number that corresponds with the cutting list at the beginning of the project. Where there is more than one size option, the piece is colour coded with a key included. This key will tell you which line to follow for each different size. Seam allowances are included for all projects but always refer to the instructions before cutting.

Transferring patterns

To transfer a pattern, first find the required size on the pull-out pattern sheet for your chosen project. Then, using dressmaker's pattern paper, tracing paper or tissue paper, trace around all edges of the pattern remembering to include all the markings **A**.

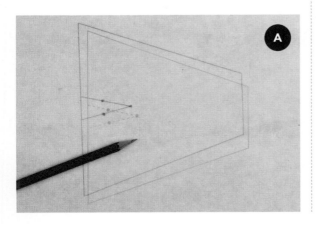

FABRIC
With the exception of fleece, most of the fabrics used throughout this book are lightweight dress fabrics such as cotton or linen. For best results, try to choose fabrics of the same weight.

The term 'fat quarter' refers to a quantity of fabric that crafters use for applique, patchwork and quilting as it comes in a handy size for cutting strips, motifs and patchwork shapes (approximately 18 x 22in/46 x 56cm). It is a different way of quartering a traditional yard of fabric so that you can get the most versatile use from it. They are modestly priced so it is easy and cheap to mix and match fabrics.

Laying out and cutting fabric

Make sure the fabric is wrinkle-free by laying it on a smooth surface and smoothing it out. Now lay your pieces onto the fabric according to the project instructions. In most cases, you will need to line up the pattern pieces with the fabric's straight grain. To do this, simply make sure the grainline arrow on the pattern runs parallel to the selvedge of the fabric.

Pin the paper pieces generously to the fabric around all edges so it can't move **B**. Use dressmaking shears to cut out each piece.

Some of the pattern pieces are shown as halves, to cut on the fold. Fold the fabric in half, in most cases along the straight grain, and align the centre fold line of the pattern along the fold of the fabric. Thus, when you cut the piece out and open it up, you will have a mirror image.

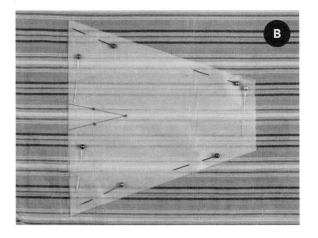

If there are left and right sides to a piece – for example, the left and right side of the elephant cot toy – cut one side, then flip the pattern over before you pin it to the fabric and cut the second side.

Pattern marks

Remember to transfer all other pattern marks to the wrong side of the fabric before you remove the pattern paper. Use a pin, tailor's chalk or water-soluble fabric marker to mark the position of buttons, pockets or any areas that require embroidery, such as eyes and so on **C**.

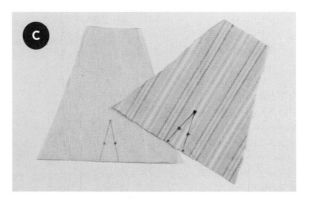

Tools

Sewing machine

This is one of the most important tools you will need. There are hundreds of different models available these days and it can be an absolutely bewildering choice for the novice dressmaker. Some are electronic, some are computerized and have embroidering options, but which one is right for you? Well, I use an ancient model passed down to me from my Nan. It has a straight stitch, zigzag stitch and a buttonhole attachment. I have a drop-in cartridge, which enables me to use other fancy stitches but, if I am being truthful, I rarely use them. A simple machine such as this has everything you need to make any of the projects in this book, at a modest outlay.

Of course, if you enjoy free machine embroidery, quilting or you love surface embellishment, then you may want to think about purchasing a machine with a computer, which will enable you to create wonderful textile masterpieces. If, however, you are a home sewer who loves to stitch home furnishings and clothes, then a mechanical machine would be a perfectly reasonable purchase to begin with.

Needles and thread

Most of the patterns in this book use lightweight dress fabrics, such as cotton (with the exception of some projects made in fleece). A universal sewing machine needle (size 10 or 12) is fine for all the projects. Remember to keep a few spare in case of breakages.

Sharp sewing and embroidery needles are essential for many of the projects in this book. A needle threader is an inexpensive, handy tool for threading machine and hand-sewing needles; it is well worth purchasing one, especially if, like me, you are short-sighted.

When purchasing sewing thread, do try to buy a good-quality one and match it to the colour of your chosen fabric. Cotton thread is best, but a good-quality polyester thread is suitable for most fabrics.

Dressmaking shears

Buy the best pair of dressmaking shears you can afford. Good quality, sharp shears can last a lifetime if well looked after and you must never use them for anything other than fabric. If you have ever tried cutting fabric with blunt scissors, you will understand the importance of this.

Other handy tools

Tape measure
Inexpensive and essential. Choose one that has both metric and imperial measurements.

Ruler
Very useful when used with a rotary cutter. Invest in a plastic, see-through one for ease of use.

Water-soluble fabric marker, fabric pencil or tailor's chalk
Choose any one of these tools for transferring balance marks from pattern to fabric. All are temporary and may be brushed off afterwards or come out with washing.

Rotary cutter and cutting mat
Excellent for fine and slippery fabrics. The round wheel is also great for cutting around corners and curves, too. Choose a gridded cutting mat for ease of use and accuracy of cutting. A must if you love quilting.

Pins and pincushion
Buy good quality sharp pins and a pincushion for holding them all in. Pins are essential for all the projects and they are inexpensive.

Seam ripper
A nifty tool that looks like a pen with a curved hook. It is very useful for opening the centre line of a buttonhole or for ripping out an incorrectly sewn seam – it can save a lot of time and frustration.

Loop turner
Not a necessity but a definite boon in the workroom. A loop turner is a long piece of wire with a hook at one end. It is used to turn narrow sewn tubes of fabric the right way out – for example, the legs of Daisy rabbit. Simply insert the hook end through the fabric tube, hook into the far end and pull the turner towards you, working the fabric right side out as you go.

Iron
Any iron will do. Just make sure you have one at all times whilst you work. My Nan's motto was 'press, press and press again'. For keeping your seams neat and your work crisp, never forget to have your iron to hand.

Machine sewing

Straight stitch

This is the most commonly used stitch in sewing **A**. It is used for topstitching, sewing seams and edge stitching. You can adjust the stitch length, but most regular sewing requires a stitch length of ³⁄₃₂–⅛in (2.5–3mm). The machine's manual should guide you.

Zigzag stitch

Zigzag stitch is commonly used along the raw edges of seams to stop them from fraying. It is also used around the edge of templates in appliqué work (see page 134) and for shirring (sewing elastic into smocking). You can adjust the width of stitch on the machine for a narrow or wide zigzag **B**.

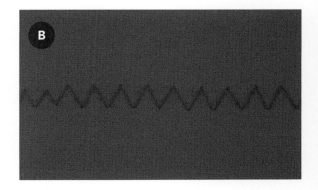

Basting stitch

These are long, loose stitches, which are easy to remove. They are used to temporarily join pieces of fabric and can be sewn by machine or by hand (see page 135). To baste using your sewing machine, adjust the stitch length to about ⁵⁄₃₂in (4mm) **C**.

Lockstitch/backstitch

Lockstitching is a very effective method of securing stitches to prevent a seam from unravelling. Position the needle a couple of stitches ahead of where you would like to begin stitching. Then use the machine's reverse button to stitch backwards to the point where you wanted to start. At the end of a line of stitching, use the reverse button again to reverse over the last few stitches of the seam **D**.

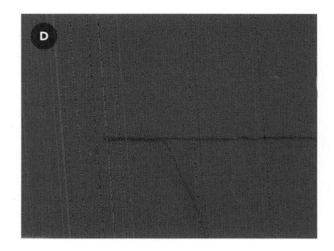

Buttonholes

Most buttonholes are worked by machine in three steps but each sewing machine is different, so consult the manual first. You will need to attach the special buttonhole foot for this technique.

1 Mark the size of the buttonhole on the fabric with a fabric marker or tailor's chalk **E**.

2 Machine-stitch a line of small zigzag stitches along each side of the marked line and close to each end by working a zigzag bar **F**.

3 Use a seam ripper or sharp scissors to open the slit between the two zigzag lines **G**.

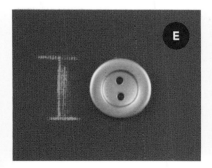

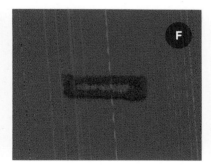

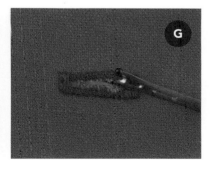

Topstitch

Topstitch is a straight stitch worked on the right side of the fabric to add a decorative finish. It can be used around pockets, for example, and is commonly seen in contrasting colours on the seams of jeans. Topstitching is usually worked close to the original seam, approximately ¼in (6mm) and parallel to the edge of the fabric **A**.

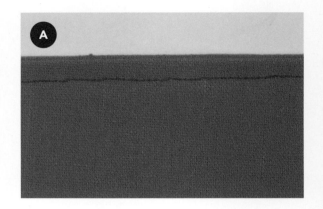

Appliqué

This technique is decorative and fun to do.

1 Trace the template onto card or stiff paper. Cut a square of your chosen fabric big enough to accommodate your template. Cut a square of double-sided fusible interlining the same size as the fabric. Lay the square on the wrong side of the appliqué fabric, adhesive side down and press with an iron to bond.

2 Place the template onto the paper-backed side of the interfacing and draw around it with a pencil. Carefully cut out the motif and peel away the paper backing. Place the motif, adhesive side down, onto the main fabric and press to bond **B**.

3 Adjust the zigzag setting on your sewing machine to narrow and test it on an off-cut of main fabric. Work a line of narrow zigzag stitch around the outer edge of the template **C**.

Hand sewing

Tacking

Tacking is also known as basting (see page 132). This stitch is used to temporarily hold pieces of fabric together and is removed when the permanent stitching is in place. Use a brightly coloured thread that contrasts with the main fabric. Thread the needle and make a knot in one end of the thread. Working from right to left, work long running stitches through all layers of the fabric .

Running stitch

This simple stitch is used to work gathers and ruffles. Thread the needle and working from right to left, work short horizontal stitches parallel to the edge of the ruffle **B**. When you have worked stitches along the whole length of the fabric, gently pull the thread to gather the fabric to the required length. Secure with a few stitches at the end **C**.

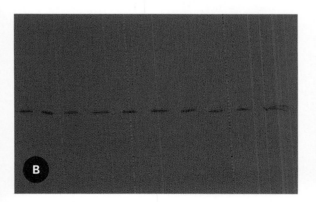

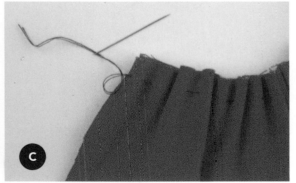

Slipstitch

This is a very useful stitch to learn. It is perfect for hemming and should be almost invisible to the eye once completed. It can also be used to close an opening – for example, when you have finished stuffing a toy. Use thread that is the same colour as the main fabric, so that it blends in. Working from right to left, slide the needle between the two pieces of fabric, bringing it out on the edge of the top fabric. Pick up one or two threads from the base fabric, then bring the needle up a short distance along on the edge of the top fabric and pull through. Repeat until you have completed the hem.

Backstitch

Working from right to left, bring needle up to right side of work at point 1, down at point 2 and back up at 3. Try to keep the distance between stitches even. Begin next stitch at point 1. Repeat as required **A**.

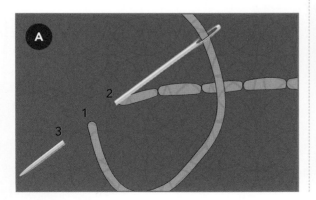

French knot

This embroidery technique can be used for making eyes and noses. Working in any direction, bring needle to right side of fabric. Holding thread taut with one hand, wind thread once or twice around needle tip **B**. Still holding the thread, insert the needle tip close to the point where you brought the needle out to the right side of the fabric and pull needle to back of work so the twist lies neatly on the fabric surface **C**. Repeat as required.

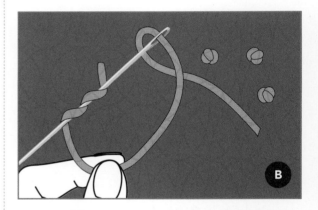

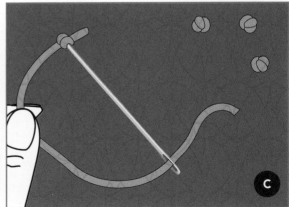

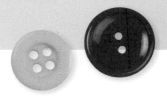

Sewing buttons

1 Thread the needle with a colour to match the main fabric. Mark the position of the button onto the fabric with a pin.

2 Using a single knotted strand of thread, make a stitch exactly where the button is to sit. Working from the right side of the fabric, sew in and out of the holes in the button until the button is secure **D**. Your last stitch should end between the button and the fabric's right side.

3 Wrap the thread several times around the sewn thread shank beneath the button. Push the needle through to the wrong side of the fabric and knot several times to secure **E**.

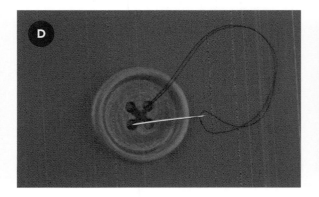

Twisted cord

Cut three lengths of yarn, three times the finished length of cord. Tie them together at each end. Hook one end over a doorknob and, holding on to the other end, walk backwards until the strands are taut. Now, twist clockwise and keep on twisting until the cord starts to fold up on itself. Keeping it taut, bring the knotted ends together. It will twist up naturally into a fat cord. Knot each end to secure **F**.

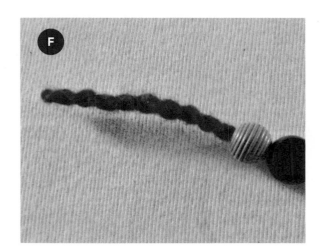

Finishing techniques

Trimming seam allowances

Trim seam allowances to get the best shape on curved edges, such as collars, cuffs and hat brims and to remove bulk. Carefully trim the seam allowances to about ⁵⁄₃₂in (4mm) **A**.

Clipping curves

To help curved edges 'behave', and to look even and crisp, it helps to clip into the seam. For inward curves, cut small slits and for outward curves, cut small notches **B**.

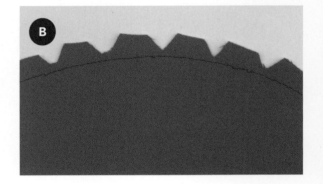

Pressing seams

Pressing as you work will help you keep seams crisp and curves neat. If you don't press, then it will make each stage harder to complete. Always press fabric on the wrong side to prevent marking **C**.

Finishing seams

To minimize the fraying of fabric, which can lead to the subsequent demise of the seam, I advise finishing all edges before you sew any seams. You can do this in several ways. The first is to use the zigzag stitch on your sewing machine to close to the raw edges of the fabric 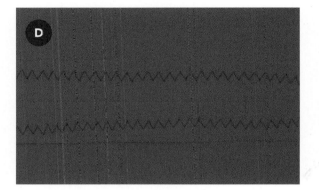.

You can also hand-sew the seams: thread a needle and work a row of stitches that enclose or over-cast the raw edge .

You may wish to invest in an overlocker (serging machine), which will give you a very professional finish. It is worth the investment if you intend to do a lot of sewing 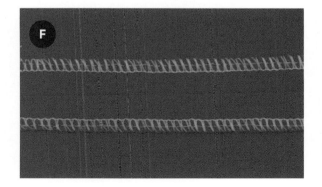.

Size chart

	0–3 months	3–6 months	6–9 months	9–12 months	1–2 years	2–3 years
height	25in (64cm)	27in (69cm)	29in (74cm)	32in (81cm)	36in (91cm)	39in (99cm)
chest	18in (46cm)	19in (48cm)	20in (51cm)	21in (53cm)	22in (56cm)	22½in (57cm)
waist	17½in (44cm)	18in (46cm)	19in (48cm)	20in (51cm)	20½in (52cm)	21in (53cm)

Suppliers

Fabric and materials

Fabric Rehab
Unit 3B
Dedham Vale Business Centre
Manningtree Road
Dedham
Colchester
Essex
CO7 6BL
Web: www.fabricrehab.com
Email: contact@fabricrehab.co.uk

Fancy Moon
51 Villa Real Road
Consett
Co. Durham
DH8 6BL
Web: www.fancymoon.co.uk
Email: customerservices@fancymoon.co.uk
Tel: 0845 519 4354 / +44 (0)1207 581923

The Cloth House
47 Berwick Street
London
W1F 8SJ
Web: www.clothhouse.com
Tel: +44 (0)20 7437 5155

Buttons and notions

Mary Goldberg Ceramic Buttons
Stockwell Farm
St Dominick
Saltash
Cornwall
PL12 6TF
Web: www.stockwellceramics.co.uk
Email: info@stockwellpottery.co.uk
Tel: +44 (0)1579 351035

MacCulloch & Wallis
25–26 Dering Street
London
W1S 1AT
Web: www.macculloch-wallis.co.uk
Tel: +44 (0)20 7629 0311

Loop
15 Camden Passage
London
N1 8EA
Web: www.loopknitting.com
Tel: +44 (0)20 7288 1160

Acknowledgments

AUTHOR'S ACKNOWLEDGEMENTS
I would like to say a big thank you to all those who made this book possible.

Thanks must go to Gerrie Purcell at GMC for having faith in me and commissioning the book in the first place. Also, thanks to Virginia Brehaut for excellent editorial skills, gentle coaxing and endless patience with me.

A huge, big thanks to Chris Gloag who took such fabulous photographs and to Gilda Pacitti who made such a wonderful job of styling the book.

Special thanks goes to all those who shared enthusiasm for the project and donated fabric, buttons and notions. A special BIG thanks to Nancy at Fabric Rehab, who donated such a generous amount of gorgeous fabric to the cause. I hope you love the finished article as much as I do.

Finally, big hugs to my ever-loving family: you inspired it all and to my children; I hope you pass some of the love down to your own families when the time comes.

PUBLISHER'S ACKNOWLEDGEMENTS
Photography by Chris Gloag, assisted by Guillaume Serve.

Thanks to the following babies and toddlers and to their mummies and daddies for allowing us to photograph them for this book: Arthur, Edith, Heidi, Vermillion, Lila, Dexter, Ethan, Sofia, Max, Jack and Otto.

Many thanks to Wickle, Lewes, East Sussex (www.wickle.co.uk) for the generous loan of props.

Index

Project names are shown in *italics*

A

appliqué 134

B

backstitch 136
Baby bibs 55
Baby's cot quilt 34
Baby shoes 111
basting stitch 132
buttons (sewing on) 137
buttonholes 133

C

Caterpillar toy 44
Changing bag 23
clipping curves 138
cutting fabric 129

D

dressmaking shears 130

E

Earflap hat 26
Easy-peasy sunhat 19
Elephant cot toy 86

F

fabric 128
fat quarters 128
finishing seams 139
finishing techniques 138
Flower garden cot mobile 66
French knots 136
Froggie hooded towel 51

H

hand sewing 135

J

Japanese doll sundress 104
Jack and Daisy rabbit 70
Jungle wall art 40

L

laying out fabric 129
lockstitch 133

M

machine sewing 132
Military shirt 120

N

needles 130
Nursing cushion 58

P

patterns and templates 128
pattern marks 129
Picnic basket & fruit 77
pressing seams 138

R

Reversible buggy liner 14
running stitch 135

S

sewing machine 130
size chart 140
slipstitch 136
straight stitch 132
Sunshine skittles 82

T

tacking 135
templates 128
thread 130
Toddler trousers 114
tools 130
topstitch 134
transferring patterns 128
trimming seams 138
Tulip dungarees 94
Twisted cord 137

Z

zigzag stitch 132

To place an order, or to request a catalogue, contact:
GMC Publications, Castle Place, 166 High Street,
Lewes, East Sussex BN7 1XU United Kingdom
Tel: +44 (0)1273 488005 Fax: +44 (0)1273 402866
www.gmcbooks.com